BATTLE STATIONS

BATTLE STATIONS

Decisive Weapons of the Second World War

Taylor Downing
and
Andrew Johnston

Pen & Sword Books Limited, Barnsley
LEO COOPER

First published in Great Britain in 2000 by Leo Cooper
an imprint of Pen & Sword Books Limited
47 Church Street, Barnsley, South Yorkshire S70 2AS

*For up-to date information on other titles produced under the Pen & Sword imprint,
please telephone or write to:*
Pen & Sword Books Limited
FREEPOST
47 Church Street
Barnsley
South Yorkshire
S70 2BR

Telephone (24 hours): 01226 734555
E-mail: sales@pen-sword.demon.co.uk
Web site: www.pen-and-sword.co.uk

ISBN 0-85052-749-X

British Library Cataloguing in Publication Data

**Printed by Redwood Books Ltd
Trowbridge, Wiltshire**

Contents

INTRODUCTION

THE MACHINES that travel on land, at sea and in the air, are built to do a job. They work – with varying degrees of success – until they wear out or become obsolete and are replaced. It's a logical and unemotional part of progress. But a few machines are born for greater things. They become symbols of their time and are enshrined in the national folklore, featuring on the stamps and the bank notes, beside the great and the good. Man-made creations like Henry Ford's *Model T* car and Charles Lindbergh's plane *Spirit of St. Louis*, Admiral Nelson's ship *Victory* and George Stephenson's locomotive *Rocket* have all become landmarks – milestones on the road to where we are now. Ford may have claimed that 'history is bunk', but he helped to shape it as surely as any statesman.

Not all the landmark machines are the passive servants of man. Some can be deadly, like the revolutionary 'Spitfire' fighter aircraft, perhaps the ultimate symbol of Britain's 'Finest Hour' in World War Two. Some make their mark in war and in peace, like the American DC-3 airliner – a triumph of civil aviation, which also became a legend on the battlefield. The 'Sherman' tank epitomises American mass production in wartime and the 'Duck' amphibian represents American ingenuity at its most inventive.

War can bring out the best and the worst in every nation, it combines the urge to create with the urge to destroy. New reserves of talent are tapped, inventions and discoveries blossom forth – shortages of vital raw materials like rubber, silk and copper, prompt new inventions like PVC, nylon and polythene. But the aim of warfare is to destroy the enemy and the sweeping advances in technology and mass-production, meant that World War Two became the most destructive conflict in the history of mankind. Vast quantities of precious resources were blown apart, incinerated or sent to the bottom of the ocean. Human life was wasted on a similar scale: when the war ended with the unleashing of another new discovery – the Atomic Bomb – it is estimated that some fifty-six million people had lost their lives.

In the 1930s, as Germany blindly followed its charismatic leader Adolf Hitler into the jaws of hell, it seemed as if an evil genius had touched the scientists and inventors of his 'Thousand Year Reich'. Britain's Prime Minister, Winston Churchill, foresaw the dawning of what he called 'a new Dark Age, made more sinister and perhaps more protracted by the lights of perverted science'. From German laboratories and workshops, there poured a steady stream of highly sophisticated technological advances. Soon Germany was far ahead of her rivals, with better aircraft, engines, tanks, ships and guns. Eventually Churchill's prophetic vision would become only too real, as Germany's scientists went on to produce better gas chambers and better crematoria – for the better disposal of expendable slave labour.

As the civilised world slowly woke up to what was happening, a sense of panic swept through its military, scientific and industrial establishments. For most European countries, the alarm call came too late and they were over-run by Hitler's war machine in days or weeks – their air forces wiped out on the ground, their obsolete defences by-passed and their armies out-gunned. Even the vast Russian superstate could not hold out against German technology and the unequal struggle would cost the lives of some twenty-eight million Soviet men, women and children. In World War Two, it was technology that held the key to victory. Britain, with her huge Empire, and America, the self-proclaimed 'Arsenal of Democracy', should have been an invincible partnership. But much of their technology was outdated and it took them years to catch up. Hitler's ambition eventually claimed the lives of approximately seven million of his own people, yet even in its death-throes, Nazi Germany was able to produce highly advanced weapons like the Me 262 jet fighter and the V2 ballistic missile.

The machines that eventually turned the tide in favour of the Allies were a combination of high and low technology. Mechanised warfare demanded every type of equipment – from highly sophisticated fighters like the British Spitfire, to the humble Duck amphibian, a solid and reliable American truck chassis, converted into a boat in just thirty-eight days. These machines represent two very different approaches to industrial design. British industry has always tended to seek quality at the expense of quantity. Inventors like to perfect their ideas, consider, modify, reject and start again, before they are absolutely satisfied. What tends to emerge at the end of this long gestation is a high-quality product with a limited market, often because it has been overtaken by events and is already becoming obsolete. By contrast, American industry will settle for second best, as long as it works. A member of the Chrysler Corporation neatly expressed the philosophy when he stated that 'in this practical nation, the engineer is disciplined by the production man and the salesman'. The priority is to get into production fast and stay ahead of the competition. With luck, the problems can then be sorted out as they arise.

War rarely turns out as planned and much of the Allied success in the Second World War depended on a rapid and open-minded response to a whole range of problems, supported by the ability to mass-produce the solutions in huge numbers – both typical of the American approach. When President Franklin Roosevelt asked America's aircraft builders for an all-out effort to produce 50,000 planes a year, Donald Douglas didn't list the problems; he confidently responded with the simple answer 'we can do it'. He not only believed in the 'American Way', he also backed it by turning out his share of aircraft, including a staggering 10,000 military transport versions of his DC-3 airliner.

What Americans call the 'Can Do' approach didn't always produce the best designs for the job, but it produced them quickly and in such vast quantities that the end result was often much the same as having fewer, better machines. If the German Tiger tank is twice as good as the American Sherman, one way to even the odds is to simply make twice as many Shermans as they have Tigers. Build four times as many and you'll probably win.

War is a mass of contradictions and conflict seems to be an essential part of evolution and progress. In the film *The Third Man*, one of cinema's most memorable speeches is delivered by Orson Welles, playing the black market racketeer Harry Lime. He points out that thirty years of warfare and terror in Italy, produced Michaelangelo, Leonardo and the Renaissance; while 500 years of peace and democracy in Switzerland, produced – the cuckoo clock.

This is the story of four machines that helped to bring victory to the Allies and roll back the Dark Age of Fascism. They may not have been great works of art, but they did mark a kind of renaissance in engineering design and they certainly weren't cuckoo clocks. All were triumphs of mass-production which would distinguish themselves in battle, and help to lay the foundations for peacetime progress.

This book accompanies a television series of the same name produced and directed by the authors for **Flashback Television**. As ever with such joint ventures there are a number of people who have contributed in a variety of ways to what follows. Without the encouragement (and the cash!) from Charlie Maday at The History Channel in the United States this whole project would not have been possible. The enormous success of The History Channel is very much down to Charlie's understanding of his market and his ability to commission quality programming. We are proud to have been linked with the Channel from its early days. Commissioning Executives Elyse Miranda and Beth Dietrich-Segarra of the US History Channel have helpfully seen us through the production process. With the UK History Channel, Geoff Metzger, Sarah Allan and Martin Morgan have been supportive throughout and their enthusiasm has been much valued.

The production team at **Flashback Television** has contributed in countless ways to this book. Paul Nelson as researcher and Aileen McAllister as film researcher have both played a major role, as has Gareth Johnson as editor. Tim O'Connor and Claire Otway as production managers have helped to make the programmes happen. (It is a remarkable coincidence that Claire is the grand-daughter of the Lieutenant Colonel Otway who led his paratroop team against the odds to storm the Merville Battery on the night before D-Day – see p. 127/8) Several other colleagues at Flashback Television have helped to make the series run smoothly. And Seimon Pugh-Jones has acted as advisor on military equipment and has expertly co-ordinated the military reconstructions with us. Henry Wilson at Pen and Sword first spotted the potential of a book to accompany the television series and to him we owe special thanks. Roni Wilkinson has worked magnificently on the design and layout of the book. He has undertaken most of the picture research and his encyclopedic knowledge of military history has proved invaluable to us. Finally, there are many veterans with whom we have spoken, in Britain and in the United States, some of whom appear in the final programmes. Their memories and experiences have greatly enhanced the text of this book, as have their personal photographs. We thank them especially.

But after many thanks to everyone above, only we can accept final responsibility for what follows. Any errors are ours.

A dedicated website accompanies this book and the television series and can be found at:

www.battlestations.net

TAYLOR DOWNING
ANDREW JOHNSTON

March 2000

The colour photographs in this book are the work of Seimon Pugh-Jones.

The majority of black and white photographs are from the extensive collection in the Taylor Library, Barnsley.

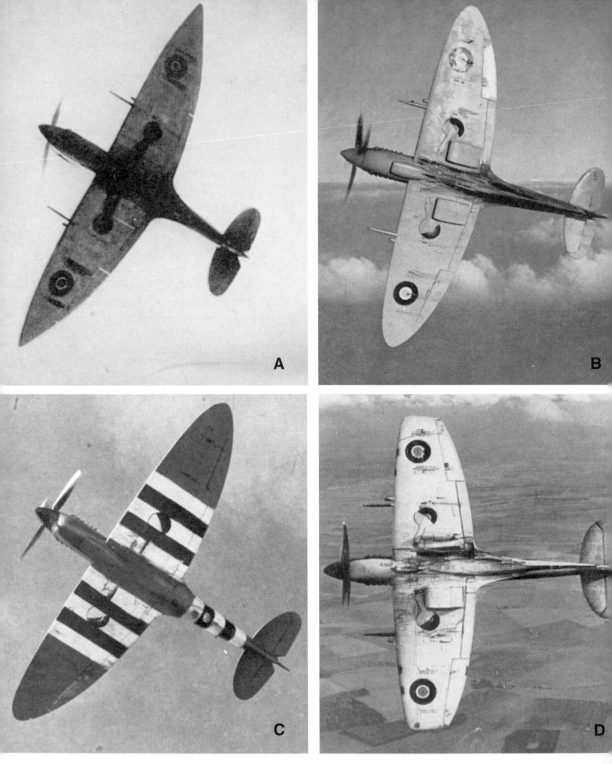

Some variations on a theme: (A) Spitfire VII, designed for high altitude work. (B) Spitfire VIII, low altitude version of the MkVII. (C) Spitfire XI, photographic reconnaissance version. (D) Spitfire XII, low altitude fighter, with the Rolls-Royce Griffon engine, and 'clipped' wingtips.

Chapter One

SPITFIRE – THE BIRTH OF A LEGEND

In the summer of 1940, Britain came closer to defeat than at any point in her history since William the Conqueror invaded in 1066. Between July and October 1940, the epic struggle for air supremacy that passed into history as 'The Battle of Britain' was fought in the sky over southern England by the young pilots of the Royal Air Force. They were pitted against the world's most powerful fleet of bombers and fighters, Germany's Luftwaffe. For the German leader, Adolf Hitler, the air battle was merely the prelude to a full-scale invasion of Britain, but it was vital to control the skies before attacking from the sea. The Luftwaffe's Commander, Herman Goering, assured his leader that shooting the RAF out of the sky would be easily accomplished in a matter of days. He was wrong, but he could so easily have been right.

In the 1930s, Britain's air defences were woefully inadequate. The Royal Air Force was small and consisted mostly of obsolete aeroplanes. By 1940, modern Spitfire and Hurricane fighters were being introduced, but there were not nearly enough of them. The Luftwaffe was well equipped and morale was high among its pilots. Most had already seen action and were used to the sweet smell of success. Whether knocking down antiquated Polish biplanes, or scattering French refugee columns, they had rarely encountered any serious opposition. When the Battle of Britain began, the RAF pilots were heavily outnumbered and badly trained. Most had been reared on thrilling adventure stories of heroic airborne duels in World War One, from which the British always emerged victorious. But this was the real thing and their chances of survival didn't look good. For many, the first taste of action was an almost unreal experience. Sergeant Pilot Bob Doe was lucky. He recalled,

> *'I found myself behind a Me 110 so I closed up on it and shot at it and I was utterly astonished when this thing turned over and dived down into the sea. I then did something you should never do, I followed him down. I saw him crash into the sea and as I pulled up I realised I was being shot at from behind and this aircraft overshot me. So I settled behind him and shot him down. So I shot down two on my first operation, without knowing what was happening around me in the sky, or who was doing what. And so in my case, it was sheer luck that I*

wasn't killed in my first action. It wasn't any skill on my part.'
Sergeant Pilot 'Bam' Bamberger came close to disaster, but survived.

'And suddenly these Me 109s flashed past, with their yellow noses. They looked killers and they looked professional and I felt very much an amateur. I saw tracer going past my aircraft and someone in the Squadron shouted 'Break', which I did. And suddenly I found myself alone in the sky and there was nobody there – not even any enemy aircraft. My aircraft was not hit and I didn't fire my guns, but I came back to base slightly wiser. The majority of the pilots who were shot down in the Battle of Britain, were shot down from behind and were taken by surprise.'

All too often, the inexperienced pilot was not given that precious second chance to learn: he fell victim to the yellow-nosed killers on his first mission. If he managed to survive that first encounter, his chances of staying alive improved dramatically. He learned to watch his back, to avoid straight and level flight during combat, to turn away from the curving lines of tracer that came darting at him from behind and how to half roll and dive out of trouble. Only when he had mastered the art of survival and could fly his aircraft by instinct, was he able to use the lethal power of its eight machine guns properly. Then he began to feel confidence – in himself and in his aircraft.

That confidence was justified. The Hurricane was not a highly advanced aircraft, but it was a robust and effective fighting machine.

By the 1890s man was off the ground in a heavier-than-air flying contraption – Otto Lilienthal pilots one of his successful gliders. All that was needed now was an engine.

It could hold its own against the most common German fighter, the Messerschmitt Bf 109, and outmanoeuvred the less numerous Messerschmitt 110. The Spitfire was a 'state-of-the-art' weapon and more than a match for the best that Germany could produce. But it was only thanks to the superhuman efforts of a few men with vision and determination, who devoted their energies to designing and building these aircraft, that the RAF was able to fight, and win, the Battle of Britain. Like the Battle of Waterloo, it was a very close run thing.

* * * *

When war broke out, powered flight was still a young science, only 36 years old. But it had come a long way and during World War Two it really took off. The RAF went to war in 1939 with obsolete Gloster Gladiator biplanes, built of wood and fabric. When the war ended in 1945, it was flying advanced, all-metal Gloster Meteor jet fighters. The years between were dominated by one of the most successful aircraft designs ever created – the legendary Supermarine Spitfire.

The story of aircraft design divides roughly into three phases: first the age of lighter-than-air balloons and un-powered gliders, then the propeller-driven age and finally the jet age. In fact each phase overlaps the next and each has involved a constant process of change and

By 1912 the military was showing a keen interest in aviation; here British Army Aeroplane model No.1, designed by Samuel Cody, is being wheeled out for a test flight. The aeroplane's value was seen to be in the reconnaissance role, spotting for the army. The classic aircraft shape had yet to emerge.

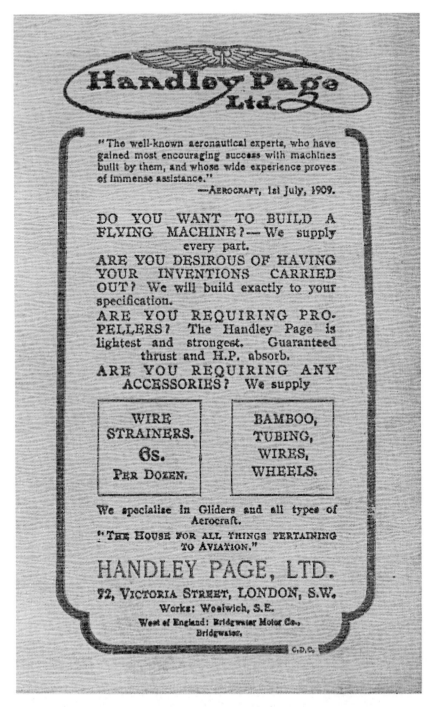

Britain's aircraft industry was born in the small workshops of pioneering companies like Handley Page. In 1909 they could supply the amateur enthusiast with 'all things pertaining to aviation'. Only thirty-five years later they were building the giant Halifax bomber for the RAF.

discovery. Although the invention of the jet engine is usually regarded as the big breakthrough that launched man's domination of the air, most of the key developments in flight actually took place during the age of the propeller.

Flight development really got off the ground when the pioneers began to understand that 'thin' air is actually a surprisingly dense medium, which can be cut into slices, pushed, compressed and ducted. When the Wright brothers made their first powered flight in 1903, they used two whirling fans to pull their machine along. The twisted blades of a propeller literally cut their way through the air, advancing like a screw thread into a block of wood, they are even known as 'air screws'.

Although the first propellers were crude, the basic design would change very little. Not so the airframe. Early aircraft were based on the existing technologies that harnessed the force of the wind: the sailing ship, the windmill and the kite. Like the sails of a windmill, aircraft used a wooden framework with fabric stretched over it. Like sailing ships, they relied on a system of rigging to brace the frame and, like the box-kite, most had two wing surfaces, one above the other.

The 'Aero Manual' of 1909 captures the pioneer spirit of the early aviators. It explains how to build your own glider at home for £3.17s.3d (roughly £3.87p). It specifies selected bamboo, piano wire and calico as the best materials and takes a wonderfully optimistic view of any risk involved:

The clean lines of the Sopwith Triplane of 1917 show just how quickly aircraft design had evolved from the ungainly pre-war machines.

'In gliding there is no danger, if one be not ridiculously imprudent and provided one is strong enough to suffer a few shocks without hurt. Impatience, rashness and precipitation are the very essence of peril, whilst, on the other hand, calmness, self-possession, patience and self-restraint will carry the gliding devotee safely and unscathed through thousands of flights.'

But even enthusiasts who possessed all these virtues still regularly ended up killing themselves. What was not properly understood was the basic principle of fixed-wing flight. Watching birds soaring for long periods, without beating their wings, the early designers assumed that they were 'riding' on the air like a surf-board. The bigger the wing area, the greater the lift, they reasoned. So biplanes were popular because their two wings added to an aircraft's lift. It was later discovered that a wing's lifting ability depends as much on its cross-section as its area, since it actually gets most of its lift from suction. Air flowing over its curved upper surface has to travel further, and becomes thinner, than the air flowing underneath its flat, lower surface. It is this difference in air density which produces the lift and, within limits, the deeper the wing, the greater the lift. But a thicker wing also presents increased resistance to forward movement, known to aircraft designers as 'drag'. More power at the propeller is then needed, but more power usually means more engine weight, which requires more lift, and so on. Aircraft design has always been based on

By the end of the Great War, aircraft designers were starting to produce streamlined designs. This captured German Albatros DIII, sporting RAF roundels, shows to advantage the spinner merged with the rounded fuselage. But the fixed undercarriage and biplane wings still created unwanted drag.

a series of compromises.

After rapid progress during the First World War, aircraft development slowed down. A glut of war surplus machines meant there were few customers for the aircraft manufacturers. But by the late 1920s, things were picking up and a few more adventurous designers were starting to abandon the biplane form and the traditional materials of wood, wire and fabric. All-metal monoplanes began to appear which used revolutionary construction techniques. The stretched fabric was replaced by lightweight aluminum sheet, closely riveted to rigid formers, also pressed out of thin sheet, which replaced the wooden frame. One unexpected bonus of using sheet metal for the frame, was its ability to acquire strength while being made lighter. A series of holes cut in a metal sheet will reduce its weight. But if the edge of each hole is belled-out to form a raised rim, the sheet becomes more rigid in the process. The all-metal combination of formers and skin produced a one-piece shell, known as a 'monocoque' – a structure which combined great strength with minimum weight. Most of its strength came from the rigidity of its skin and no bracing wires were needed.

One of the first designers to see the potential of the new technique was Reginald Mitchell. He was chief designer for Supermarine, a small company based in Southampton, which built seaplanes. In 1927, Mitchell hit the headlines when his Supermarine S5 racing seaplane

Still defending Britain with a fabric body and an open cockpit! Hawker Harts, two-seater RAF fighters of the 1930s incorporating obsolete design and construction techniques from the Great War. New aircraft types were urgently needed.

won the prestigious 'Schneider Trophy' for Britain, against strong international competition. The trophy was awarded to the fastest aircraft competing over a measured course. His design was highly advanced, with a streamlined fuselage creating the minimum of drag, a huge engine and thin wings. He repeated his triumph in 1929. It was a condition of the trophy that any nation which won it three times would retain it permanently and everybody expected a third British bid for victory. But in 1930, the Labour government decided it should not be spending taxpayer's money on air races and withdrew funding.

Into the breech stepped an aristocratic saviour. Lady Lucy Houston announced that she was 'utterly sick of the lie-down-and-kick-me attitude of the Socialist government. I live for England and I want to see England always on top,' she said. (It was common among the aristocracy to refer to England when meaning Britain). To prove the point, she offered £100,000 of her personal fortune to fund a third attempt. It was an astronomical sum for a private individual to give. At a time when a new family car cost less than £150 and a modest house could be bought for £300, it represented the equivalent of many millions at today's prices. But events were to prove that it was money well spent. Reginald Mitchell's new seaplane design, the S.6B, swept to victory and briefly touched the unheard of speed of 407 mph. Lady Houston and Reginald Mitchell became the heroes of the hour. The triumphant aircraft was hailed by the press, by the British public and by the pilots of Britain's Royal Air Force.

Into the future. The sleek, all-metal Supermarine S.6B of 1931 designed by Reginald Mitchell.

During the First World War, the British army had established an air force, the Royal Flying Corps. As its importance grew it was given the status of an independent service. In April 1918, the Royal Air Force was born, joining the Army and the Royal Navy as a key member of Britain's armed forces. But the new service had inherited many of the more entrenched and conservative views of the military establishment and failed to move with the times. While Mitchell's S.6B seaplane of 1931 had briefly exceeded 400 mph, the RAF's front line fighters could barely manage 200 mph. Their pilots might dream of flying a fighter as fast as the S.6B, but the Air Chiefs who wrote the rule books and dictated policy on fighter design knew better. In their view, speed was less important than manoeuvrability in a traditional dogfight and many experts firmly believed that an agile biplane could always out-turn and defeat a faster monoplane. Mitchell took the opposite view. He was convinced that the key to victory in the air was speed. He was not alone: in Germany designers like Ernst Heinkel, Hugo Junkers and Willy Messerschmitt were also developing their ideas for fast fighter and bomber monoplanes.

In 1931, Britain's Air Ministry issued F.7/30, the specification for a design to replace its Bulldog biplane fighter. Aircraft companies were invited to submit proposals and Supermarine decided to try

The old order. An early attempt at a monoplane fighter, the Bristol Bullfinch, with thick, fabric covered wings and little regard for streamlining. Inset, the Bristol Bulldog, in service with the RAF but obsolete by 1931.

their luck. This was a new field for the company, their reputation had been built on seaplanes and they lacked the capacity for any large-scale order. But they had recently been taken over by Vickers, a major player in the aviation industry, with a large factory located within the famous Brooklands race track at Weybridge in Surrey. Mitchell submitted a design which was based on his S.6B seaplane, but stuck closely to the Air Ministry brief. It had an open cockpit, fixed wheels and large wings, kinked above the wheel struts, giving it the head-on outline of a flattened 'W'. It was a surprisingly ungainly machine compared to the S.6B and its Rolls Royce Goshawk engine gave it insufficient power. It was soon obvious to Mitchell that his metal monoplane design was little better than the traditional biplanes it was meant to replace and it was withdrawn. The contract was eventually awarded to another biplane design, the Gloster Gladiator.

In 1932, Rolls Royce began privately developing an advanced engine, known as the Private Venture, or PV-12. It used light-weight materials and was designed to produce up to 1,000 hp, with the aid of a supercharger to blow air into the massive 27 litres of its twelve cylinders. Mitchell realised that this engine could offer the extra power he needed, while its small frontal area would minimise the drag. But he also saw that his original airframe had been wrongly conceived. By sticking closely to the Air Ministry brief, he had produced a compromise between their traditional thinking and his own, much

The Heinkel He100, one of many all-metal monoplanes developed in Germany during the 1930s. Despite its record-breaking flight in 1939, the design lost out to the Messerschmitt Bf109.

more advanced, ideas. He resolved to try again and, with the backing of Supermarine, began work on a new design. But he began to feel seriously unwell and cancer of the colon was diagnosed. After a major operation, he went to Europe to convalesce. Meanwhile, Germany's newly-elected Nazi Government was secretly planning a powerful new air force – the Luftwaffe. Soon designers like Heinkel, Junkers and Messerschmitt began developing a new breed of fast, all-metal monoplanes. As Adolf Hitler tightened his hold on power, his military ambitions became clearer. Some in the British aircraft industry began to suspect that another war with Germany could be on the horizon. Mitchell was still frail after his operation, but he set to work on his fighter design with renewed determination.

What emerged on the drawing board was a work of genius. Mitchell's new design was bold and entirely original. Its clean lines gave it the long, low appearance of a racing machine. The wheels retracted into the wings giving it a highly streamlined shape. The wings themselves were very thin, to create the minimum drag, but they were extremely strong. They had a 'D' section leading edge of thick sheet metal and a complex spar built up from a series of box sections of decreasing size, fitting one inside the other like a Russian doll. What Mitchell had produced was a jet-age airframe, at a time when much official thinking was still stuck in the era of the box-kite.

Breaking the mould is rarely an easy task. The new technology was regarded with suspicion by the defenders of the biplane and by many

The complexity of the airframe revealed in Mitchell's drawings. These show the wing attachment points.

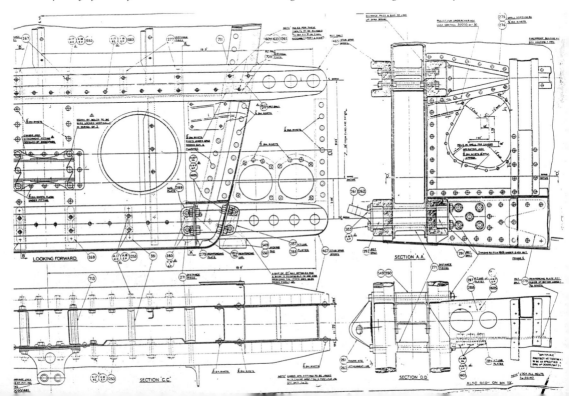

of the engineers who would have to mass produce it. Tried and trusted methods and materials would have to be discarded. As with the motor industry's change from coach-building to welded steel, traditional crafts like woodworking, rigging and fabric skinning had to be replaced by the metal press, the power drill and the rivet gun. But Mitchell had the ability to inspire his team with his vision of the future and they set to work on the prototype airframe with a sense of growing excitement.

It was normal practice to design aircraft wings with straight edges, tapering towards the tip. In them Mitchell would have to fit the folding wheels and the four machine guns which the Air Ministry required any new fighter to carry. Biplanes had always mounted their guns on the fuselage, usually above the engine, since this was the strongest point and best able to absorb the recoil. But since this meant firing through the propeller arc, synchronising gear had to be fitted to ensure that the pilot did not blast his own prop blades to matchwood when he opened fire. Mitchell's wings would need the strength to accept two guns apiece, firing outside the prop. But then there was a change of policy. All new fighters were now to be fitted with eight guns, to inflict the maximum damage in the two or three seconds that it was estimated that accurate fire could be held on a target during airborne combat.

Mitchell had been considering the advantages of a wing with

The nerve centre of the Spitfire was the pilot's instrument panel. The position of every switch and dial was carefully planned.

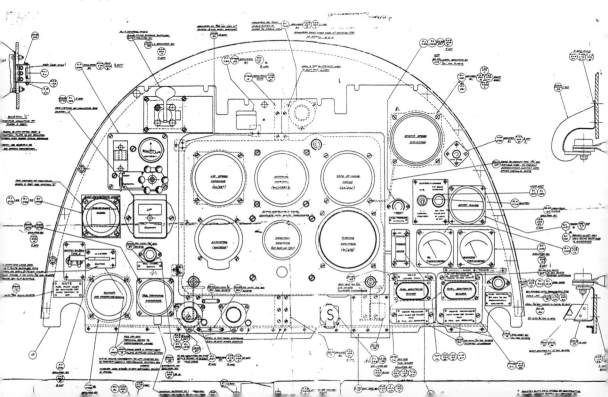

curved, rather than straight edges. It offered greater area than the more normal straight taper, but without the need to make the wing thicker. It also provided the extra room needed for more machine guns. The elliptical wing design which evolved on Mitchell's drawing board would set the seal on the Spitfire's success as a fighter, while at the same time creating its most beautiful and most identifiable feature. Slowly the airframe began to take shape, as the detailed drawings were translated into metalwork.

Meanwhile, the new Rolls Royce engine had been through its testing and emerged with flying colours. Following the company policy of naming engines after birds of prey, it was christened the Merlin. In early 1936, the Merlin was fitted into the finished airframe of Mitchell's prototype fighter, known simply by its works number K5054. On 5 March 1936, Mutt Summers, chief test pilot of the Vickers company, climbed into the tiny cockpit of the new fighter at Eastleigh Airfield, near Southampton. A small group of Supermarine staff, including R. J. Mitchell, had gathered to see the historic first flight of K5054. After a short run, the aircraft left the ground safely and its flying career began. After 15 minutes Summers landed and pronounced it satisfactory. The first hurdle in the race to develop a fighter that could meet the German threat, had been overcome.

It was decided that the new fighter must have a name. Supermarine had proposed to call Mitchell's first (unsuccessful) design the 'Spitfire'.

The hallmark of the Spitfire, Mitchell's graceful elliptical wing, takes shape on the drawing board.

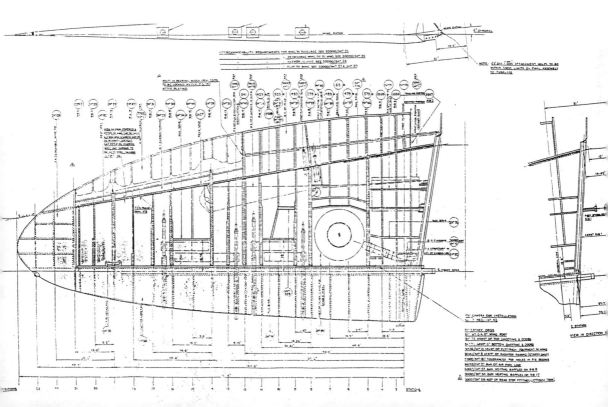

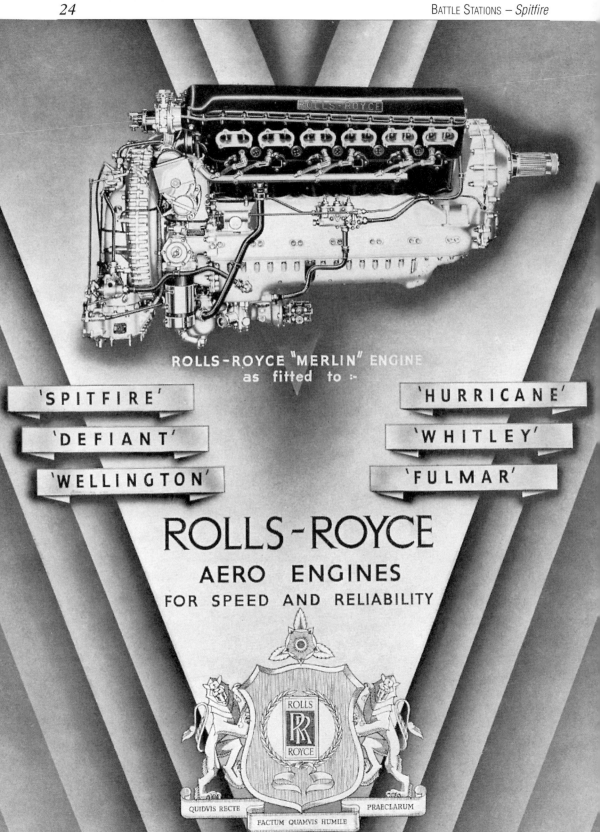

ROLLS-ROYCE "MERLIN" ENGINE
as fitted to :-

'SPITFIRE'   'HURRICANE'

'DEFIANT'   'WHITLEY'

'WELLINGTON'   'FULMAR'

ROLLS-ROYCE

AERO ENGINES

FOR SPEED AND RELIABILITY

QUIDVIS RECTE   PRAECLARUM

FACTUM QUAMVIS HUMILE

Now the name was revived by the company bosses and applied to K5054. Mitchell had painful memories of his previous failure and was not enthusiastic about the choice. 'Sort of bloody silly name they would give it,' was his caustic comment on the birth of a legend.

After its initial flights had proved satisfactory, K5054 was passed to Supermarine test pilot Jeffrey Quill. He soon developed a conviction that the aircraft was destined for great things, but it clearly had its faults. The first problem was its speed. At 330 mph it was fast, but not as fast as Mitchell, or the Air Ministry had hoped. The manual pump for raising the wheels was awkward to operate and the forward vision was very poor on the ground. The narrow wheel track also made it unstable on the uneven grass airfields which it would have to operate from. Another problem was the control surfaces.

The basic elements of an aircraft like the Spitfire are fairly simple: the engine and propeller to make it go, wings to make it fly, fuselage to accommodate the pilot and a tail unit to give stability. The other essential feature is control. On the tail fin, a rudder keeps the machine in line, while hinged elevators on the tail plane make it dive or climb. Flaps under the wings increase the lift for landing and hinged ailerons nearer the wing tips, tilt the aircraft for turning and rolling. Since high-speed combat depends on fast manoeuvers, it is vital that a fighter should have positive and responsive controls. In the 1930s, even designers as far-sighted as Mitchell still believed that fabric covering was needed for control surfaces, to keep them light. On the Spitfire, it had exactly the opposite effect. Although its speed in level flight was rather disappointing, its speed in a dive was awe-inspiring, thanks to the thin wing section. But, as the air flow over the wing's top surface neared supersonic speed, the fabric covering of the ailerons would be sucked out of shape, making them almost impossible to move. The answer was simply to make them of metal, like the rest of the aircraft.

In almost all other respects, the Spitfire was a delight to fly, with a

Left: *the key to victory in the Battle of Britain was speed, as delivered by the high performance Rolls-Royce 'Merlin' engine. Later in the war it was replaced on the Spitfire by the larger 'Griffon'.*

Below: *Launching a revolution – the very first Spitfire, K5054. Its only visible link with the past is the tail skid for use on grass airfields.*

forgiving nature. This was largely due to the exceptional flying qualities of Mitchell's wing. Below a certain speed, a wing will no longer generate enough lift to hold up an aircraft. At this point, known as the stall, the wing will literally stop flying and drop like a stone. If he has sufficient altitude, a pilot can probably recover from a stall. As the aircraft goes into a dive and speed builds up, the wing soon reaches flying speed and he can normally regain control. But a stall can easily flip an aircraft on its back, if one wing drops first. In extreme cases, it can develop into every pilot's worst nightmare – a flat spin, in which all control is lost and the aircraft rotates rapidly while falling out of the sky. In aerial combat, high speed turns are essential to avoid an attack. But fast turning can also produce stalling conditions. As the aircraft tips over on its side, the steeply banked wing progressively looses its ability to generate lift and the pilot can find himself dropping out of the turn and into a dive. Mitchell's understanding of flight dynamics produced a fighter which would warn its pilot before he got into trouble. By including a subtle twist in the shape, he created a wing which stalled later at the tip than it did at the root. The aircraft would begin to shudder as the stall began, but it went on flying and gave the pilot a chance to take avoiding action.

By May 1936, a change of propeller and other detailed improvements, had raised the Spitfire's speed to 348 mph. Mitchell had wanted 350, but it was enough. The prototype was passed to the Air Ministry for testing and, although its fighting abilities were still unknown, an order was placed for 310 Spitfires on 3 June 1936. 600

'I climbed into the cockpit and Ken Scales helped me to fasten my parachute, then closed the little access door at shoulder height. The cockpit was narrow but not cramped. The instrument panel was tidy, symmetric and logically laid out. At once I felt good in that cockpit. I primed the Merlin engine carefully and it started first time and from the stub exhausts, one for each of the 12 cylinders, came a good powerful crackle whenever a small burst of power was applied for taxiing. I did my cockpit checks. With a last look round for other aircraft I turned into wind and opened the throttle. The aircraft tended to roll on its narrow undercarriage, but soon we were airborne and climbing away. At once I had to reset the rudder trimmer and then to deal with the undercarriage retraction and the canopy. The undercarriage had to be raised with a hydraulic hand pump, so it was necessary to transfer the left hand from the throttle to the stick and operate the pump with the right, difficult to do without inducing an oscillation of the whole aircraft.

'However, once fully airborne the aircraft began to slip along as if on skates with the speed mounting up steadily and an immediate impression of effortless performance, somewhat reminiscent of my old Bentley cruising in top gear. The view straight ahead was almost non-existent as one got close to the ground, so I approached the airfield in a gentle left hand turn, canopy open, and head tilted to look round the left-hand side of the windscreen. As I chopped the throttle on passing over the boundary hedge, the aeroplane showed no desire to touch down – it evidently enjoyed flying – but finally it gently settled on three points. Here, I thought to myself, is a real lady.'
From 'Spitfire' by Jeffrey Quill

The cockpit of an early Spitfire. On the left can be seen the control column, with the firing button for all eight machine guns. On the right is the awkward hydraulic hand pump used to raise the undercarriage.

Hurricanes were also ordered. With the threat from Germany becoming more obvious every day, it was not a moment too soon. But the fact that twice as many Hurricanes had been ordered, was an indication of problems ahead. The Spitfire had still not been fitted with guns and a number of senior members of the RAF and the Air Ministry had serious doubts about its suitability. While the solid and workmanlike Hurricane designed by Sidney Camm was the latest in a series of successful military aircraft, Mitchell's design came from a racing stable and looked the part. Was this sleek and elegant creation really a fighter, or another racer? Within the company, there were also worries. Many of the people working with Mitchell seriously doubted if Supermarine could cope with building more than three hundred examples of such an advanced machine.

The Supermarine company had no experience of building such a large batch of combat aircraft, its previous designs had all been seaplanes, and their biggest order to date had been for 79 Southampton flying-boats: much larger than the Spitfire, but much less complicated to build. To produce, in sheet metal, the curved shapes of Mitchell's design would involve elaborate construction techniques. Jigs would have to be set up as templates, within which the airframe could be built to exact dimensions. The wings, in particular, would prove a nightmare to mass-produce. In the days of fabric covering, the material could be stretched to fit round awkward shapes involving compound curves, like wing tips. Sheet metal will bend easily, but in one direction only. So fixing a panel to the curved

THE HURRICANE
   The same Air Ministry specification F.7/30 that eventually produced the Spitfire, also sparked the creation of the other fighter that was to play a key role in the Battle of Britain – the Hawker Hurricane. Between the wars, the Hawker company had built up a solid reputation for building successful, single-engine biplane fighters and bombers. But when their Chief Designer, Sidney Camm, produced designs for F.7/30, they were rejected as too conventional. The contract went to the Gloster Gladiator, another biplane design and just as conventional as Camm's proposals. Like Mitchell, Camm then set out to create his own design, ignoring the restrictions of the Ministry brief. It was based on his existing 'Fury' biplane fighter. By removing the top wing and re-designing the lower one, he produced a monoplane which retained many of the traditional features of the biplane. It used an inner framework of metal tubes, braced with wires. A wooden frame was then built up round the metal structure, with a fabric covering stretched over the top.
   The result was a strong and easily serviced airframe, able to withstand a lot more battle damage than an all-metal monocoque. The German Fighter Ace Adolf Galland complained that he could expend all his ammunition shooting large pieces off it, but it would go on flying. Christened the Hurricane, it used the same Rolls Royce Merlin engine as the Spitfire and had several advantages over its rival. Firstly it was much easier, cheaper and quicker to build than the Spitfire. It was easier to handle on the ground since Camm had designed the Hurricane's wheels to fold inwards, giving it a wider track. This also allowed the guns to be grouped close together, just beyond the propeller arc.
   The Hurricane played the leading role in the Battle of Britain and accounted for roughly two thirds of all kills, but this does not automatically mean it was the better fighter. Because it was quicker and easier to build, there were far more Hurricanes than Spitfires available in the summer of 1940. The faster-climbing Spitfires were increasingly sent up to tackle the German fighter escorts, while the Hurricanes concentrated on shooting down the slower-moving bombers. Most pilots who flew both types agree that the Hurricane was a practical and rugged tool for the job, but lacked the brilliance and performance of the Spitfire. It was really a bridge between the old biplanes and the era of high speed, high power machines which soon became the jet age.

top of a wing is simple. But try also bending that curved sheet round to form a pointed wing tip and the problems start. The metal refuses to co-operate. It creases and folds up like a squashed tin can – it may even split, to relieve the stresses produced. The untidy solution is to make up the compound curve from small, overlapping segments. The best method is to hammer or press the metal into shape.

As with a steel car body, convex shapes are much stronger than flat sheets, but they are awkward and expensive to produce. Had the Spitfire's wings followed the conventional tapered shape, their mass-production in metal would still have been a demanding job for a company like Supermarine. But Mitchell's elliptical wings were a riot of curves, with barely a straight line to be seen anywhere!

As the exhausting programme of testing continued, Mitchell devoted all his remaining energy to the project. But his health was failing rapidly. Medical tests established that his operation had not halted the spread of his cancer and he knew he had very little time left. He was now in constant pain as he fought to finish his task. The strain had taken its toll; he was barely forty, yet photographs show the face of a man of sixty. As the tests continued, Jeffrey Quill became more and more certain that the Spitfire was a vitally important aircraft. A close bond developed between him and Mitchell as they collaborated on the smallest details of performance. A

minor modification, a test flight, a detailed report, another modification – and so on. No detail was too small to consider, even the humble rivet. Mitchell had designed an absolutely smooth surface for the metal skin of his fighter. This meant that every single rivet hole had to be countersunk to take the flat-headed flush rivets. But were they all essential? With tens of thousands of holes to make on every single aircraft, much time and labour (and cost) could be avoided during production by the use of conventional dome-headed rivets. To establish what drag would be created by domed heads, the design team went out shopping. Several bags of dried split-peas were bought from a local grocer and one was glued to the head of every single rivet, creating the effect of a domed head. Flight testing revealed a loss of 22 mph on the top speed. By progressively scraping off row after row of peas, the lost speed was regained, while the critical areas that needed flush riveting were identified: the rest could stay dome-headed.

On 18 June 1936, the Spitfire was demonstrated to the press. Although the flight was cut short by engine problems, the headlines were ecstatic. 'The fastest military aircraft in the world' proclaimed *The Times*. It was a publicity triumph for Mitchell and Supermarine, but behind the scenes, progress was painfully slow. It was another six months before the prototype Spitfire began weapons testing and there was no hope of getting into production in the near future. Mitchell's declining health meant that he was seen less often at Eastleigh and the

Prototype K5054 gets the 'once over' from officers of the Royal Air Force.

project began to slip badly behind schedule. By March 1937, a whole year after its first flight, K5054 remained the only Spitfire in existence. On 22nd March, an engine failure occurred in flight. Fortunately, the pilot was able to crash-land in open country, with very little damage to the airframe, but it further delayed the testing programme. In May, Mitchell returned from visiting Europe's leading bowel cancer specialist, who confirmed that his illness was terminal. On 11 June, 1937, he died. He was just 42 years old.

The loss of its leader was a devastating blow to the Spitfire team. But the crucial years between his cancer operation and his early death had seen his design progress from the seed of an idea, via long hours at the drawing board, to an outstanding and beautiful aircraft. Against the odds, he had managed to achieve his dream of producing a fighter which could defend his country in its hour of danger. His vision had been passed on to the rest of the team and his deputy, Joe Smith, was able to keep them together. They faced a long haul before all the problems of production were solved, but they remained true to Mitchell's design and the aircraft which finally went into production was his.

Meanwhile, the international situation was rapidly worsening. Germany's military build-up was now too strong to halt without open war. All that Britain could do was to buy time and step up its production of arms. An emergency was fast becoming a crisis and on

At long last, the Spitfire was on the production line. The tubular framework in front of each cockpit will carry the Merlin engine.

3 May 1938, the British government increased the Spitfire order by 200 to 510. The aircraft was still an unknown quantity, but – apart from the Hurricane – it was the only hope of avoiding going to war with a fleet of hopelessly outclassed biplanes. Twelve days later, on 15 May 1938, the first production aircraft was test flown. But the Air Ministry was in no mood to celebrate the fact. Almost two years had passed since the contract had been signed. Deliveries were supposed to have begun in October 1937 and the original contract for 310 was due for completion by March 1939. It was obvious that Supermarine had a lot of catching up to do, but the complexity of the design suggested there would be even more delays to come.

The Men from the Ministry expressed their dissatisfaction in no uncertain terms, while conveniently forgetting their own contribution to the problem. The run-down state of the Royal Air Force in the 1930s meant that the aircraft industry, starved of military orders, was in no position to suddenly mass-produce an air force that should have been planned much sooner. The British aircraft industry would eventually expand its labour force by no less than 4,000%, to more than 1,800,000 people, but in the late 1930s, the process was only just beginning. Winston Churchill had constantly warned the government of the German threat, but he was a lone voice in a Parliament hostile to talk of re-armament. The belief that World War One had been 'The War to end all Wars' ran very deep and the Government could claim with some justification that by neglecting defence, it was simply reflecting the mood of the nation. Supermarine and its parent company Vickers,

THE MESSERSCHMITT Bf 109

The standard German fighter throughout the war was developed from the pre-war gliders designed by Willy Messerschmitt. The Bf 109 was an outstanding aircraft with some very modern refinements and good performance, which closely matched the Spitfire and outclassed the Hurricane.

Like Mitchell, Messerschmitt believed in monoplanes with thin, low-drag wings. But unlike Mitchell, he still stuck to the biplane-era tradition of mounting the guns on the engine, which he inverted to provide space. His wings were certainly thin, but were not really strong enough to carry the loads imposed by high speed combat. Nor were they designed to carry guns. When two wing-mounted cannon were added as an afterthought, they could only just be squeezed into the limited space.

Metal aircraft design had been pioneered by the Germans. As early as 1915, Hugo Junkers had produced an all-metal monoplane and Messerschmitt continued the process with the Bf 109's advanced, all-metal monocoque airframe. But it lacked the strength of the Spitfire: the tail planes had to be braced with struts and the wheels had to be hinged out from the fuselage, to avoid over-loading the wings on landing. The result was an undercarriage even narrower and less stable than the Spitfire's. An unwary pilot could easily tip the aircraft onto its wing. Some five percent of all Bf 109s were lost in accidents on the ground.

Cockpit access and visibility were also unsatisfactory. The cockpit cover hinged at the side, which made bailing out very awkward. Its thick frame reduced the all-important visibility and many German pilots fell victim to unseen attackers. Although outclassed by later fighter designs, the Messerschmitt 109 became the most numerous fighter in the history of flight, with an astonishing 33,000 examples built by the end of the war in Europe.

now became convenient scapegoats for its lack of vision.

It was not possible to concentrate all the Spitfire production at the Supermarine factory in Southampton. The limited workshop space meant that work would have to be sub-contracted out. It was decided to build the fuselages in-house and to sub-contract wing production to other companies. Final assembly would be done by Supermarine. This system got off to a very shaky start. The wings were probably the most complicated section to manufacture and the sub-contracted work was soon well behind schedule. Wing-less fuselages began to accumulate in rows at the Supermarine works, while frantic efforts were made to sort out the problems. An official inspection of Supermarine during mid 1938, found 78 fuselages in the factory, but only three sets of wings.

One positive event during this depressing period was the modification of a Spitfire for an attempt at the World speed record. In trials, this aircraft reached 408 mph, not enough to take the record, but proof that the Merlin engine could be 'doctored' to produce a spectacular power output. The standard Merlin produced roughly 1,000 hp, but the modified engine was able to produce over 2,000 hp for short periods on special fuel. It was a pointer to the future, which would see huge increases in power and speed, to levels undreamed of in the early days. Mitchell's successor, Joe Smith, became convinced that the Spitfire held the potential for almost unlimited development. Rather than try to design a replacement, he believed the company should stick with Mitchell's original and inspired creation.

But there were plenty who disagreed with Smith's vision of the future. As the delays and production problems mounted up, the Air Ministry had become thoroughly disenchanted with the aircraft. In June 1939, it was proposed to call a halt to Spitfire production, once the contract for 510 had been completed. There was talk of Supermarine being given other designs to build. The bureaucrats tended to see the Spitfire as a problem, rather than an asset. Future development possibilities were ignored and it would take the Battle of Britain to show how wrong they were.

Meanwhile, Spitfire production had finally got into its stride and by the time war broke out in September 1939, Supermarine were delivering ten aircraft a week and the RAF had just over 300 machines ready for action. A large new factory was established at Castle Bromwich near Birmingham. It was run by the head of the Austin Motor Company, Lord Nuffield. His brief was to mass-produce Spitfires, using his experience as a mass-producer of cars. But cars are not aircraft and working on a design as sophisticated as the Spitfire was not the ideal training ground for motor mechanics. By September 1939, they had not produced a single finished aircraft. In May 1940 Britain's new Prime Minister, Winston Churchill, created the Ministry of Aircraft Production. Its first minister was Lord Beaverbrook, a newspaper proprietor with no experience of aircraft production, but boundless energy and determination. His first priority was to sort out the chaotic situation at Castle Bromwich. Control of the factory was

Duxford, north of London, was the first fighter station to receive the new Spitfires. Note the original, fixed-pitch, twin-bladed propellers.

passed to Vickers and after a few heads had been knocked together and a new organisation put in place, production got underway.

Soon the chief test pilot at Castle Bromwich, Alex Henshaw, was hard put to keep up with the output. Each new Spitfire had to be test flown, before it could be delivered for operational service. Although they were all identical in theory, many needed slight 'tuning' of the flight controls before they would fly straight and level. The testing could be very dangerous work and Henshaw experienced several engine failures in flight – and survived some spectacular accidents. But, like Jeffrey Quill, he was inspired by the flying qualities of Mitchell's creation and acquired a reputation for performing seemingly impossible feats with the aircraft. When Winston Churchill came to inspect the factory, Henshaw's dazzling display of low-level aerobatics left him in no doubt that the Spitfire was a winner.

By mid 1940, three Hurricanes had been built for every Spitfire and by July 1940 there were 19 operational Spitfire squadrons and 38 Hurricane squadrons in Fighter Command. But, largely thanks to Beaverbrook's re-organisation, Spitfire output began improving rapidly and had soon doubled. At last, the Spitfire's traumatic childhood was over. The fully-fledged aircraft began to make its mark. As its builders finally mastered the new generation of airframes and the pilots discovered what Mitchell's design was really capable of in combat, the Spitfire legend was born. But it was only just in time. Events in Europe soon threw the Spitfire and the Hurricane into a deadly combat.

Chief test pilot Alex Henshaw discuses the finer points of the Spitfire with Prime Minister Winston Churchill, during his official visit to the Castle Bromwich factory.

Chapter Two

SPITFIRE – SQUADRON SCRAMBLE

There was a hard, driving rain from the south-west as the sun came up on 10 July 1940 but the day soon cleared to become dry and cloudy. Later, this day would be marked as the official first day of the Battle of Britain. France, Belgium and Holland had been overwhelmed by the power and the ferocity of Hitler's *Blitzkrieg* (lightning war) in a matter of six weeks. With memories of four years of fighting along the Western Front in the First World War, when the front line barely moved back or forth more than a few hundred yards, the impact of Hitler's victory was immense. The French had pleaded for further air support from the RAF which was authorised by the new Prime Minister Winston Churchill, appointed on the day the German assault on France was unleashed. Air Chief Marshall Sir Hugh Dowding, head of Fighter Command argued against over-extending the RAF in the Battle of France, lest resources to defend Britain were depleted. But Churchill overruled him for political reasons. The RAF suffered badly at the hands of the Luftwaffe. In the battles of France and Norway, the RAF lost 959 aircraft of which 386 were Hurricanes and sixty-seven were Spitfires. Moreover, hundreds of precious pilots were killed,

The sight every Luftwaffe fighter pilot learned to fear – a Spitfire attacking from behind.

missing or captured.

Worse still, under constant strafing and bombing from German planes, many in the army blamed the RAF for failing to protect them. Although the reality was that the RAF were battling it out in the distant skies trying to prevent the mighty German Luftwaffe from getting anywhere near the army units, this was invisible to those on the ground. The reputation of the RAF fell to its lowest ebb and there were many reported incidents of soldiers coming to blows with airmen when they met in the street, blaming them for their defeat. But the cold facts of the battle of France made for depressing reading. Although 338,000 British and Allied soldiers were evacuated from the beaches of Dunkirk, most of their heavy weaponry and equipment had been abandoned. And of the 261 Hurricanes sent to France, only sixty-six returned to Britain. When Churchill proclaimed that 'the Battle of Britain is about to begin', RAF fighter strength was disastrously low and the whole British Isles were woefully defended. British military resources had been massively depleted by the battles in France and Belgium.

Many people, including a high proportion of the establishment, felt that it would be impossible to defeat the overwhelmingly powerful forces of Hitler's Third Reich. One general wrote to another 'Do you realise that for the first time for a thousand years this country is now in danger of invasion?' A senior civil servant wrote in his diary 'My reason tells me that it will be almost impossible to beat the Germans and the probability is that...we shall be bombed and invaded.' But

FIGHTER PILOTS

The fighter pilot has always been regarded as a romantic figure. From *Biggles* to *Top Gun*, he has been destined for stardom. The first fighter pilots were mostly members of a social elite with its roots deep in military tradition. The pilot was the natural successor to the Medieval knight in shining armour. Gentlemen were always set apart from the foot soldiers by the fact that they went to war mounted on horseback. They were collectively known as the 'Chivalry', from the French word for horse - cheval. As warfare changed, the knight's heavy armour was discarded, along with the heavy cart horse needed to carry him. The 'Chivalry' became the 'Cavalry'. Mounted on his fast, light horse, spear or sabre in hand, the Cavalry Officer was dashing, heroic, always in the thick of battle - until World War One. Behind the hellish mudbath of the trenches of the Western Front, cavalrymen still practised their horsemanship, waiting in vain for the glorious breakthrough cavalry charge that never came.

Among the Cavalry were wealthy gentlemen who had dabbled in the new sport of flying before the war. Frustrated by the lack of action on horseback, many decided to try the Royal Flying Corps. Their wood and canvas steeds were temperamental and spirited creatures which needed a light touch on the controls and it was widely believed that a good horseman would make a good pilot. Airborne combat was regarded as an acceptable alternative to the cavalry charge, a cross between a duel and a pheasant shoot.

Between the wars, the Royal Air Force continued to foster this elitism. Pilots were expected to be officers, recruiting campaigns referred to them as 'Cavaliers of the Skies', members of the great 'Freemasonry of the Air'. They were taught to fly their antiquated 200 mph biplanes in tight, neat formations and to regard themselves as a breed apart and an invincible force. When the 350 mph Spitfires first entered this fantasy world, the brighter pilots suddenly realised how much catching up was needed. Many lives would be lost before some of their senior officers fully understood that the whole 'game' had changed.

Winston Churchill was determined that there would be no surrender and no negotiation of terms with Hitler. When the German Fuehrer made a speech in the Reichstag indirectly appealing for Britain to come to the negotiating table, many in Britain thought this would be the most sensible course of action. In Cabinet, the Foreign Secretary, the Earl of Halifax, argued for a negotiated peace. But Churchill refused even to respond to the German leader's appeal, on the grounds that he 'was not on speaking terms with Herr Hitler'. Churchill was reassured by secret communications with American President Franklin D. Roosevelt, who perceived that it would not be in US interests for the whole of northern Europe, including Britain, to fall under Hitler's sway. Roosevelt, without the support or even the full knowledge of Congress, and bypassing his ambassador in London, Joseph Kennedy, pledged support to Churchill and hoped that Britain would not be defeated in the great struggle that was bound to follow. This added extra determination to Churchill's natural bulldog spirit.

On 16th July, Hitler issued Fuehrer Directive No 16 in which he declared:

> *'As England, in spite of her hopeless military situation, still shows*
> *no sign of willingness to come to terms, I have decided to prepare, and*
> *if necessary to carry out, a landing operation against her.'*

Preparations had to be completed by 16th August. Later in the war, the Allies would need nearly two years to plan a combined invasion of occupied France, the other way across the Channel. And that was with all the men and materials supplied by the great arsenal of the United

States at their command. The Germans had barely a month. It was an impossible challenge.

Goering had already taken the initiative and ordered the Luftwaffe to attack the RAF 'by day and by night, in the air and on the ground'. Fresh from his successes in France and Belgium he hoped to wear the RAF down by a process of attrition and by demonstrating overwhelming air superiority to convince the British that further resistance was useless - making the invasion, code named Operation Sealion, unnecessary. So, in July 1940, Goering's Luftwaffe began to harass shipping in the English Channel and to attack ports in southern England. The Battle of Britain had begun.

In a series of magnificent speeches, Churchill began to rally the people of Britain. In words redolent of Shakespeare's Henry V on the eve of the battle of Agincourt, Churchill called on the people of Britain to 'brace ourselves to our duties, and so bear ourselves that, if the British Empire and its Commonwealth last for a thousand years, men will still say 'This was their finest hour'.'

Without the Spitfire and Hurricane, Churchill's stirring words would have been little more than empty rhetoric. Defeat would have been swift and certain. No matter how brave and determined they were, the RAF pilots would have stood little chance against the Luftwaffe. The new fighters came just in time – and so did their new propellers. Both the Spitfire and the Hurricane entered service with two-bladed, fixed-pitch, wooden propellers – a legacy of the biplane

OPERATION SEALION

In his militaristic vision of a Greater Germany, Hitler had never conceived of the need for an invasion of Britain. And in the summer of 1940, having conquered all of northern Europe he thought the British, with whom he had no real enmity, would seek an honourable peace rather than risk the humiliation of defeat. When it became clear that Churchill would not consider negotiating terms, Hitler was forced to act. General Franz Halder, Chief of Staff of the German Armed Forces Supreme Headquarters, was made responsible for the invasion of Britain code named Operation *Seelöwe*, Sealion. But Halder saw the invasion as little more than a river crossing on a broad front, ignoring the fact that the English Channel can be one of the world's roughest stretches of water.

A plan was drawn up in which 260,000 men, fresh from their stunning blitzkrieg victories over France, Belgium and the Low Countries, would land on the beaches of southern England. Six divisions would land between Ramsgate and Bexhill, four between Brighton and the Isle of Wight, with a flank attack from Cherbourg in Lyme Bay. The invasion front would span some 200 miles. The objective was that within a few days, reinforced by massive panzer armoured divisions, most of southern England would be occupied in a line from Maldon on the Essex coast to Bristol in the west. London would be surrounded and would soon surrender. It was estimated that the rest of the country would be taken within a month. Pretty English village high streets would become battlegrounds, the Home Counties would become a giant combat zone with a front line running across its 'green and pleasant land'.

But Grand Admiral Erich Raeder, the German naval commander-in-chief, objected to this plan. After suffering heavy losses in the Norwegian campaign, the German Navy could not match the firepower of the Royal Navy. Raeder told Hitler that he had insufficient protection for an invasion across such a wide front and could not guarantee security for the German invasion fleet as it crossed the Channel. He feared that the Royal Navy might destroy his fleet before a single German soldier had set foot on English soil. Hitler, however, overruled Raeder. Operation Sealion was to proceed as planned.

era. The German aircraft had three-bladed, variable-pitch propellers. The pitch, or angle of the blade, needs to change in flight to extract the maximum performance from the engine. Much as a car needs to start in low gear for maximum power, a propeller needs to be in 'fine-pitch', (taking small slices of air) on take-off. For high-speed flight it performs best in 'coarse-pitch', taking much bigger bites with each revolution of the prop. A fixed-pitch blade is always going to be a compromise setting between the two. Just before the battle began, a rushed programme of 'retro-fitting' new, variable-pitch props with three blades was carried out on all Spitfires and Hurricanes. It produced a marked improvement in performance, clipping crucial seconds off the rate of climb and increasing the all-important top speed.

For the pilots, that first encounter with a Spitfire was a memorable experience. Bob Doe was posted to a typically ill-equipped squadron which still trained its pilots on First World War biplanes. He later recalled,

'Then one day a Spitfire landed on the airfield and taxied over to our hangar. We all rushed over to this thing and walked round it, stroked it, sat in it. I know I fell a bit in love with this aeroplane – it was beautiful. And then fifteen more turned up and we were a fighter squadron!'

It was love at first sight for most pilots, but that was only the beginning, the first date. When he was firmly strapped into his seat and the engine was started, the romance really took off.

Converted Rhine barges did not make ideal assault landing craft. Some 2,000 river barges were assembled at French ports for the cross Channel invasion of England. Air superiority was vital for Operation Sealion to have any chance of success.

'Once you got it into the air, it was a dream. You didn't fly it, you were part of it. My shoulders touched both sides of the cockpit and my head was about a quarter of an inch from the roof at the top, so you were part of the aeroplane. You weren't just sitting in it, you were part of it. That was the beauty of the thing. If you wanted to turn, you thought about it – and you turned! It was a dream.'

Clearly the Spitfire was far more than just a machine. Just as the cavalryman bonded with his thoroughbred charger, the pilot became one with this thrilling new creation. 'If it looks right, it'll fly right' is a common expression among pilots and the Spitfire looked better and flew better than anything they had ever met before.

As the Battle of Britain began in July, the RAF were outnumbered by the Luftwaffe roughly two to one. In terms of fighter planes though, the two sides were more evenly matched. Fighter Command had about 500 serviceable Hurricanes and Spitfires whereas the Luftwaffe possessed around 650 Messerschmitt Bf 109s ready for action. (Approximately 700 Hurricanes and Spitfires were available in all versus 800 Bf 109s and 250 Messerschmitt Bf 110 twin engined fighters.) And Beaverbrook had made dramatic improvements in the rate of construction of new fighters to about 400 new planes a month – enough to replace all those shot down and damaged. But the young pilots on whom Britain's destiny now depended, were well behind the German pilots in terms of tactics and experience. The Luftwaffe had learned many lessons through its involvement in the Spanish Civil

AIRCRAFT ARMAMENT

Cinema has helped to create many myths about warfare. The Hollywood image of fighter pilots unleashing a constant stream of gunfire is as far from reality as the Wild West shoot-out, in which each 'six-shooter' seems to hold at least a hundred rounds. Combat during the Battle of Britain was usually a series of brief flashes of action in a rapidly changing and confused melee. Bursts of fire usually lasted no more than two or three seconds.

The British fighters were armed with eight Colt Browning machine guns, four in each wing. Each gun was fed by a belt of 300 rounds, giving about 15 seconds of fire. But the guns were only .303 in calibre, the same as an army rifle, and although delivering 20 rounds per second from each gun, only about four pounds weight of bullets would be fired in total per second. Firing at long range, or with badly aligned guns, this limited firepower could be spread so thinly that unless a fuel tank or the pilot himself were hit, the effect would probably not be fatal.

Pilots could specify what ammunition should be loaded by their armourers. There were four types in common use: ball (or plain) shot, armour-piercing, incendiary and tracer. The normal distribution was ball in four of the eight guns, armour piercing in two and incendiary in the remaining two. Each ammunition belt contained tracers in the final 25 rounds as a warning to the pilot that he was about to run out. Some pilots liked a mix of ammunition types in each gun. Within a belt of ball shot, every fifth round was often an incendiary. They could be highly effective if a fuel tank was hit and produced a flash on impact, which showed the pilot when his shots had struck home.

An early discovery was that guns could easily freeze up in the sub zero temperatures encountered at high altitude. One solution to this was the ducting of hot air to the guns from the engine. The Hurricane and Spitfire armourers soon found that canvas taped over the gun ports would help to keep out moisture until the moment of firing. The sight of blackened and tattered canvas patches on the wings of returning aircraft would instantly tell the ground crews if their pilot had been in action and often provoked a triumphant cheer.

Although the Messerschmitt Bf109 carried only a pair of light machine guns on the engine, its two wing-mounted cannon fired heavy 20 mm explosive shells and a single hit from one of them could be deadly. But, with only 60 rounds per gun, the pilot had little scope for error. His supply of shells would be exhausted in about eight seconds.

War in the late 1930s and these lessons had now been refined in the skies over Poland, Norway, Belgium and France. They flew in formations of four, called a Schwarm, which the RAF pilots called the 'finger four'. These could easily break into pairs of two leading planes each with a wingman. Moreover, their battle experience had taught the Luftwaffe pilots the importance of maintaining height over enemy planes being attacked and the value of attacking with the sun behind you so as to appear 'out of the sun' to the pilot under attack. Many of these lessons had been learnt the hard way during the aerial dogfights of the First World War but somehow had been forgotten by the RAF during the peaceful interwar years.

Squadron commanders of the RAF almost without exception adhered faithfully to the Fighter Area Attack Manual, the bible of the pre-war Air Force, now hopelessly outdated. This called for squadrons to fly in four flights of three planes in a close-knit V formation. The pilots spent more time ensuring they were flying correctly in formation with their leader than scanning the skies around them for enemy planes. It was later claimed that a pilot needed to spend 45 seconds out of every minute looking behind and around him. This was impossible when the rule was to fly in close formation. When one aircraft was detached from the formation to watch its rear it did little good. By weaving from side to side this pilot used up his fuel much more quickly and then himself became a vulnerable target. Furthermore, Fighter Command tactics were based on the assumption

that their fighters would be attacking defenceless bombers who had flown from airfields in Germany. There were no German fighters with the range to fly this far and accompany the bombers. However, when France fell the Luftwaffe was able to relocate its airfields into northern France, only thirty or forty miles from the English coast. So the formations which confronted the RAF fighters in the summer of 1940 consisted of bombers often backed by a large fighter escort which, flying alongside and above the bombers, could swoop down on a flight of attacking Spitfires and Hurricanes and wreak havoc. The fall of France fundamentally changed the rules for the RAF who were far too slow to catch up with the reality of this new game. Rigidly holding on to outdated regulations cost the RAF many young lives in the combat that would follow.

Britain now stood alone against the Nazis who occupied all of northern Europe, with only the Channel as a barrier to an immediate attack by German forces. So the first phase of the Battle of Britain, from 10th July to 11th August, consisted of concerted German attacks on shipping in the Channel. Despite poor and overcast weather, mounting waves of bombers and dive bombers attacked convoys as they rushed through the narrowest point at the Strait of Dover, where the Channel is barely twenty miles wide, which became known as 'Hellfire Corner'. The Germans mined the shipping lanes and bombed nearly all the ports of southern England. The fighter escorts tried to flush out the RAF fighters and to draw them into combat but Dowding was reluctant to be drawn, trying to preserve his numbers for what he

Bob Doe, later to become one of the leading RAF aces in the Battle of Britain, said of the training that led to his first action:

'We did everything wrong that we could possibly do wrong. We'd had no information on what tactics to use. There'd been a thing called the Fighter Area Book on tactics, which showed you what formations to use when attacking formations of bombers. No mention of what happened if you met a fighter or anything like that. And when we went into action for the first time, we flew off in close formation, which is the most stupid thing you can do, because it means the only person not formating is the leader, so there's only one person looking around. We'd go up to the same height that we were told the enemy were, which again is fairly stupid: you want to be above them. We proceeded to patrol up and down the sun, which was idiotic, because half the time you can't see a blind thing behind you.'

knew would be sterner tests ahead. On 19th July, the RAF lost six of its Defiant fighters in combat with Messerschmitt Bf 109s. Even with their rear turret guns, the slow moving Defiants were no match for the German fighters and the RAF defensive plan now became increasingly focused on the two legendary fighters, the Hurricane and the Spitfire.

Despite Dowding's caution, RAF losses continued to grow. On 25th July, the weather improved and with clearer visibility the Germans mounted a series of attacks on Channel shipping. By the end of the day, 11 merchant ships and two naval destroyers escorting the convoys had been sunk or disabled. On the same day the RAF lost six aircraft and the Germans sixteen. At last it was decided that convoys would only sail through the Channel at night. But still the aerial battles grew bigger almost daily. 50 Stuka dive bombers with about twenty-five Bf 109 escorts attacked on the 29th July.

Meanwhile, preparations for Operation Sealion continued. Without landing craft, the German army scoured the inland waterways of western Europe looking for barges – the only flat-bottomed vessels they could find to make beach landings. These were assembled in Dutch, Belgian and French ports. Some were specially adapted to carry tanks and other heavy vehicles. But with so much to be done, it soon became clear that Sealion's deadline of August 15th could not be met. On the last day of July, Hitler held a conference at his Bavarian retreat, the Berghof. Raeder once again advised a narrower invasion front and recommended that the invasion of Britain should be postponed until May 1941. Hitler was not pleased, but he pushed back the date for the

MARKSMANSHIP

A fighter aircraft is only as good as its firepower. The fastest and most responsive combination of airframe and engine will be no use in battle if it cannot shoot down its opponent. Like battleships, fighter aircraft are often referred to as 'gun platforms'. Stability and strength are vital if the machine is to shoot straight and withstand the recoil. Flight and gunnery are conflicting activities, which cause constant problems. An aircraft in flight is not an easy target to hit, even from a static gun platform. Shots must be aimed ahead of it if they are to intercept it. The process, known as deflection shooting, involves complex calculations based on the target's speed and course and on the velocity of the projectile. When the gun platform is itself an aircraft, also moving at speed, the calculations become even more complex.

Today, deflection is predicted by computers: during the Battle of Britain, it was down to the pilot's ability to think fast in three dimensions. His only help came from the reflector gunsight, mounted ahead of him in the cockpit. This early example of the 'head up' display used in modern fighters, showed him a circle of light, containing a central dot. While watching his target through the gunsight, he could still see the dot and ring. The distance between the two represented a crossing speed of about 50 mph and gave him some help, when trying to predict deflection. The inclusion of tracer bullets in the ammunition also helped, although they often simply told the pilot how far off target he was. Many of the best pilots turned out to be surprisingly poor marksmen. Again and again, fighter pilots in the Battle of Britain would open fire at long range, only to see their line of fire curving away uselessly, far behind the target.

As they became more experienced, pilots realised the vital importance of 'harmonising' their guns to ensure that all were focused on a single point and of getting in as close as possible before opening fire. The effective range of the Browning .303 machine gun was 3,000 ft, but combat experience soon demonstrated that this was not the ideal harmonisation point. Most preferred about 900 ft and the better marksmen would focus their guns at half this distance. This reduced the delay between firing and scoring hits, while increasing the concentration of the hits and the velocity of the bullets.

invasion to 15th September.

The deciding factor on whether Sealion would go ahead or not depended on Hermann Goering and his Luftwaffe. The planners recognised that an invasion on this scale could only succeed if Germany ruled the skies over southern England. So in August 1940, the Luftwaffe prepared a concentrated attack to destroy the Royal Air Force once and for all. During prolonged attacks on 8th August, 160 enemy aircraft were counted in the action. The RAF lost 15 planes; the Luftwaffe 21. And three days later, the Germans launched mass attacks against Dover and then Portland. The tally for this day was 30 RAF fighters to 35 Luftwaffe losses. At this loss rate, the RAF faced the appalling prospect of total extinction within six weeks.

Although the RAF pilots were outnumbered and still adhered to poor tactics in the air, they had several advantages over the Luftwaffe. Most of these came down to the efficient organisation of the RAF defence system on the ground. Fighter Command had its forward eyes in a set of early warning radar stations along the coast of Britain (still at this stage called RDF, Radio Direction Finding – the American term radar did not come into popular usage until 1943). Each station consisted of twin sets of giant transmitter and receiver towers at the base of which was located a 'receiver hut'. Here, highly skilled operators, often from the Women's Auxiliary Air Force (WAAFs) stared at cathode ray tubes. Radio signals were sent out across the sea and if they hit an aircraft they bounced back and created a pulse, or blip, on the tube. A careful measurement of the time it took for the

Air Chief Marshall Sir Hugh Dowding was known as 'Stuffy' to his staff. He was a self-opinionated man, a loner who did not socialise in the way most senior military officers did. He made many enemies, probably often without realising it. He fell out with Churchill over sending fighter aircraft to defend France in the spring of 1940. And many of his colleagues found him difficult to work with. But his quiet patience and determination, and his vision of how future air battles would be fought laid the basis on which the RAF went to war in 1940.

Dowding was the eldest son of a Victorian headmaster and he grew up in a conventional middle class family. After school at Winchester, he joined the army in 1899 and served as a gunner in several outposts of the empire around the world. Just before the outbreak of war he learned to fly and in 1914 was assigned to the Royal Flying Corps. He rose to be a Squadron Leader and then Brigadier. In 1918 he joined the new Royal Air Force and after the war Dowding continued to rise through the ranks. In charge of Supply and Research he was convinced that the future would lie with all-metal rather than wooden aircraft. And it was he who gave the necessary encouragement to the rapid development of radar.

In July 1936 he was appointed first Chief of the brand new Fighter Command. His drive to re-quip the Air Force with the latest generation of single wing fighters created the shape of the Force on the eve of war. But it was a race against time, with never enough money or resources. Part of his achievement, too, was to create the structure within which Fighter Command operated during the Battle of Britain – with radar stations and observers reporting in to a centralised network of command headquarters from which decisions would be made and passed on, and aircraft controlled.

radio wave to go out and come back could suggest the distance of the enemy aircraft. Their direction could be assessed in general terms by taking cross-bearings from two neighbouring stations. The system was primitive by comparison to the polished sophistication of later radar systems and it was often only through the calculated guesses of watchful operators that enemy aircraft were ever identified. Once the planes crossed the British coast, radar was of no use as it only pointed out to sea. Then, the RAF were reliant upon the Observer Corps. Through a variety of listening and watching devices, these volunteer observers picked up and reported back detailed information about the whereabouts of enemy aircraft, helping to guide the fighters to their targets. With their field glasses, portable telephones and charts to identify enemy and Allied planes, without uniforms and sometimes with only a tin helmet, the Observer Corps grew in numbers to about 50,000 at the peak of the Battle of Britain. Their reports on the movements of enemy raiders overhead were vital to the efficient fighting of the Battle.

This vast mass of information was fed back to the Operations Room of RAF Fighter Command Headquarters at Bentley Priory, situated in an old convent at Stanmore, in north-west London. Here, the information was filtered through a team of telephone operators and when verified was plotted on a huge table-map of Britain. This was the rapidly beating heart of Fighter Command where teams of highly trained young men and women, wearing headsets and receiving constant instructions, moved coloured markers around the table. Each

Reichsmarschall Herman Goering was the charismatic leader of the Luftwaffe and Hitler's right hand man. Although popular with his pilots he was not a strategist or someone who really understood about the technology of modern aerial warfare. The failure of the Luftwaffe in the summer of 1940 was very much a failure of leadership.

Badly wounded in the trenches in the First World War, he somehow managed to get himself qualified as a pilot and went on to become one of the most famous aces of the war. He won the coveted Pour le Mérite medal and succeeded Baron Manfred von Richtofen as commander of his famous 'flying circus'.

Goering joined the Nazi Party in 1922 and with his aristocratic origins added much needed respectability to the Party. He was the only Nazi with a distinguished military record and he soon became Hitler's Deputy and in 1932 President of the Reichstag. After the election to power of the Nazi Party he held a series of senior roles within the Party and the state as Minister of the Interior and head of the Gestapo secret police, and as the minister in charge of the four year economic plan. But it was as Field Marshall and Minister of Aviation that he was at his most dazzling and ebullient. He led the re-arming of the Luftwaffe and its transformation into a formidable fighting machine that, after the fall of France in June 1940, was at the height of its success.

After its failure in the Battle of Britain, the Luftwaffe also failed to distinguish itself in the Battle for Russia. Goering ended up reliant upon drugs and a pale shadow of his former self. He was one of the most senior Nazis captured in 1945 and was put on trial at the Military Tribunal at Nuremberg. There he regained some of his former vitality and insisted that the trial was a sham, nothing more than a victor's court to punish the defeated under the guise of a false legitimacy. Found guilty of war crimes and condemned to execution, he cheated the hangman by committing suicide with poison.

one represented an enemy force with its estimated size and height, or an RAF squadron that had been scrambled to intercept it. On a first floor balcony around the room, as from the dress circle of a theatre, the commanders looked down on the show below and took crucial strategic decisions on deploying resources and calling in reserves. From here air raid warnings were issued, and anti-aircraft gunners and searchlight teams were mobilised. Dowding always tried to be present during a raid and he would sit at his desk overlooking the whole operation giving instructions and passing on his views.

From Bentley Priory, information about enemy raids was passed on simultaneously to the four Fighter Groups that each controlled a sector of the United Kingdom. Each of the four Groups had its own operational headquarters, which in essence was a copy of the Command HQ at Bentley Priory. In addition to the local table-maps recording enemy action, on the walls around these rooms were lists of squadrons itemised in different stages of preparedness. Those in one column were standing-by at two minutes readiness; the next row listed those at five minutes; the next, those that were available in twenty minutes. Other lists on the wall kept a tally of the squadrons airborne; red lights for those in action and another row for those returning to base. Each Group headquarters had operational control over its sector and decided when to scramble a squadron and when to call for reserves. To a visitor, the scene in these control rooms would have appeared calm and controlled. But beneath the quiet tension the stakes could not have been higher. To miscalculate and over-react could have

caused great losses to the sparse resources of the RAF and risked defeat. To under-react could mean an enemy bomber force would arrive uninterrupted at its target and cause mayhem. The fate of the nation hung on the decisions made in these RAF command rooms.

For the whole Fighter Command operation, speed was essential. It could take German bombers only five minutes to cross the Channel once they had been picked up on radar. But it could take fifteen minutes for a Spitfire squadron to reach its attacking height. Squadrons were encouraged to practise scrambling in order to be airborne in two minutes from receiving the order. During the long summer days, pilots and groundcrews had to be ready from a half-hour before dawn, which came around 4.30 am, to a half hour after dusk at about 9.00 pm. Pilots would sleep, not in their quarters but in the area around their aircraft known as 'dispersal'. Often they would keep their pyjamas on and wear their flying gear on top. Soon the strain of being almost constantly on stand-by and of flying up to five missions a day was beginning to tell. An aching tiredness began to affect every pilot in Fighter Command. But this was still only the beginning.

However, it soon became clear that RAF Fighter Command did at least have one substantial advantage over the Luftwaffe – a fighter that was beginning to strike fear in the hearts of the German crews. The Spitfire was proving itself in action, often coming off better than the fighters escorting the German bombers. The remarkable achievements of Mitchell and his design team now began to show in the field of

RAF FIGHTER COMMAND STRUCTURE

The largest of the four Fighter Groups was 11 Group which covered south eastern England under Air Vice Marshall Keith Park. 11 Group was in the front line throughout the Battle of Britain. Further north, 12 Group under Air Vice-Marshall Trafford Leigh-Mallory controlled the skies from Cambridgeshire to the north of the midlands. 13 Group controlled the area from roughly north Yorkshire northwards including the whole of Scotland. And in the south and west, 10 Group was lead by Air Vice Marshall Sir Quintin Brand. At moments of particular pressure, one Group could call on a neighbouring Group for reinforcements. This system with its complex mass of communication links and hundreds of miles of telephone cabling, worked well throughout the Battle. It was a masterpiece of organisational planning that had largely been created under Dowding's supervision between 1936 and the eve of war. Later in the Battle major areas of disagreement would emerge, especially between Park and Dowding on the one hand and Leigh-Mallory on the other, over the scale of deployment and response. But at this stage the whole operation worked smoothly in marshalling the RAF's slender resources to maximum effect.

battle. The Spitfire was no faster than the Messerschmitt Bf 109 but it was highly manoeuvrable and pilots had better all-round vision out of its clear cockpit. It wasn't perfect, but even its faults became part of its character, evidence that it was a living being with a personality rather than an assembly of sheet metal, forgings, castings and rivets. The Spitfire 'talked' to its pilot, warning him when it was unhappy with his handling, the slight shudder that said 'any more of this and I'll stop flying' saved many a pilot's life. In combat, these qualities are always critical. Air fighting is about positioning the gunsight and predicting the deflection, the flying must be instinctive. With a machine as sensitive and as eloquent as the Spitfire, the RAF had an instant advantage. Once the pilot had overcome his initial sensations of trepidation, relief, wonder and elation, he was confident in a way that few pilots of other types could ever be. Often it was that confidence which gave the Spitfire pilot the edge over his opponent in the claustrophobic Bf 109.

The confidence felt by the Spitfire pilots, however good their aircraft, is surprising considering the extra handicaps of their equipment. A combat scramble during the Battle of Britain was not simply a case of running to the aircraft, jumping in, starting up and taking off. Each Spitfire pilot wore a parachute harness and parachute, which formed his seat cushion in the cockpit. Over this he wore an inflatable 'Mae West' life jacket, as much of the fighting took place over

A Czechoslovakian officer serving in the RAF explains the workings of the Spitfire to some of his fellow countrymen who are serving as ground crew.

the English Channel. He needed to maintain radio contact with his leader and his leather helmet was fitted with bulbous earphones while a microphone was incorporated into the oxygen mask that was clamped across his face. Oxygen was needed above 10,000 ft if the pilot was to breathe easily and at high altitude he would quickly lose consciousness without it. He also wore goggles, usually pushed up off the face while the cockpit canopy was closed, but vital when exposed to the blast of air from the propeller. His Sutton seat harness had to be tightly secured if he was to avoid hitting the cockpit roof when inverted during a loop or roll.

Strapped and plugged into his seat, oxygen and radio, he was ready to fly but always mindful of the need to cast it all off when bailing out in a emergency. As protection against the bitter cold encountered at high altitude, standard flying kit included a big and cumbersome sheepskin jacket, heavy lined boots and thick leather gloves, worn over thin silk inner gloves. Most fighter pilots during the Battle of Britain preferred to live with the cold and wear lighter, less restrictive clothing. Anything that came between the pilot and his controls could affect his flying. Like the cavalryman, the pilot needed to keep a light touch on the reins of his spirited thoroughbred. Heavy handed movements with an aircraft as sensitive as the Spitfire could instantly send it off course.

Survival during aerial combat depended on twisting the head

A Spitfire pilot in full flying kit ready for combat.

round constantly, to scan the sky for hostile aircraft. Pilots quickly found that the jacket, collar and tie of the RAF uniform, rubbed the neck raw and were quite impractical to wear on sorties. Most preferred to wear a jersey and a silk scarf, some even wore a lady's stocking, borrowed from a wife or girlfriend, to protect the neck from the constant chafing.

On some airfields commanders were sticklers for discipline and insisted everything must still be done by the rule book. Pilots were told they had to wear a collar and tie in the mess and mealtimes proceeded rigidly to schedule even if all the planes were out on a sortie and no pilots were there to eat. But slowly, on most airfields as the Battle unfolded, commanding officers began to turn a blind eye to minor misdemeanours and to allow pilots to adapt regulations as it best suited them.

It was during this first phase of the Battle that German plans for Operation Sealion became more clear. Hitler ordered his army generals to draw up plans for an invasion of Britain. Firstly, though, Hitler looked to Herman Goering to pave the way for an invasion. Goering happily boasted that his Luftwaffe would bomb the RAF into oblivion. Hitler and his generals knew that no landings could take place until the Luftwaffe had total mastery of the skies over southern England – otherwise the RAF would cause havoc to both the naval ships bringing the invaders across the Channel and to the army units once they had

Some of the most determined fighter pilots in the RAF were Poles, who escaped when their country was overrun, and were hungry for revenge.

waded ashore. This same principle was well understood by the Allies when they prepared their own invasion of Hitler's fortress Europe four years later. Goering assembled his air commanders and eagerly began to plan *Adlerangriff*, Eagle Attack, a massive onslaught designed to give the Germans the necessary air supremacy over Britain.

Early on the morning of 12th August the next phase of the Battle of Britain was ushered in when the Germans launched a series of attacks on the RAF's radar stations. With radio towers soaring up to 360 feet into the air, they stood out as obvious targets. Attacks on two radar installations in Kent failed to disable them. But the station at Pevensey near Eastbourne was hit badly and several operators, male and female were killed or wounded. At Rye and at Ventnor on the Isle of Wight the radar stations were put out of action but only temporarily. Through the gap torn in the radar screen, a force of some 100 Ju 88s attacked the RAF airfield at Hawkinge, overlooking Folkestone, at teatime. Hangars and sheds were destroyed and the runway was pitted with bomb craters but somehow it continued to operate. Other forward fighter stations at Lympne on the hills overlooking the Romney Marshes and at Manston, almost on the cliff edge of the Kent coast, were also attacked on this day. The attacks on Manston, which continued over the next few weeks, were so severe that the airfield ceased to be operational in all but name. Dowding refused to close it formally for reasons of morale and to avoid giving the enemy a

Pilots from 65 Squadron at Manston. **Left to right:** *'Hank' Hancock, 'Nicky' Nicholas, 'Ski' Drobinski, 'Dave' Glaser, Sgt Tabour, Sgt Colin Hewlett.*

propaganda victory, but many of the groundcrew were badly shaken and retreated into the air raid shelters.

The attacks on the radar stations were intended to open up the RAF defences for the main onslaught on the following day, 13th August, Goering's much heralded *Adlertag*, Eagle Day. Goering sent a command to every unit: 'Within a short period you will wipe the British Air Force from the sky. Heil Hitler.' The signal was immediately deciphered by the code breakers at Bletchley Park. But the day began almost farcically for the Luftwaffe. Awakening to heavy cloud cover, Goering himself issued the order to recall the first wave of fighters and bombers which had already set out across the Channel. The fighters had new crystal radio sets installed and received the order to turn back. The bombers with old radio sets, did not. The fighter commander unsure of what was happening, flew his Bf 110 across the front of the bomber commander waving frantically to turn back. The bomber pilot put this down to high spirits and carried on. The bombers now flew on unaccompanied. They caused extensive damage to bases at Sheerness and Eastchurch. But without fighter escorts they received a heavy mauling from the Spitfires and Hurricanes which were scrambled to intercept them. Five German bombers were shot down and six were severely damaged. The German bomber commander was furious and when he landed, Field Marshall Albert Kesselring came out of his bunker personally to apologise for the foul

Goering begins his campaign against England with a rousing speech to his much vaunted Luftwaffe pilots and crews.

up.

However, later in the day as the clouds began to clear the order to restart *Adlertag* in earnest was given. A German force of some 300 planes assembled with the objective of hitting the RAF airfields. They were deadly accurate in their bombing of Detling airfield. Sixty-seven airmen were killed on the ground and many planes were hit. It was a great success but for the fact that poor intelligence had misidentified Detling as a fighter base. In fact it was a Coastal Command airfield. The losses were severe but had no impact on the Battle of Britain. Elsewhere, the RAF fighters did well. Out of a force of nine Stuka dive bombers sent to attack the airfield at Middle Wallop in Hampshire, six were shot down. At the end of Eagle Day, the Luftwaffe had lost 45 planes in action; the RAF had lost 13 fighters in the air and 47 aircraft on the ground, only one of which was a fighter.

Goering withdrew to his Prussian hunting lodge at Karinhall east of Berlin, 500 hundred miles away from the action, to review the outcome of *Adlertag*. He ordered his senior commanders to join him, all of whom now left the fighting zone to travel to Goering's country estate. Goering lived an extravagant lifestyle, which added to his reputation but distracted him from the task in hand. His failure to grasp the key elements of contemporary military strategy made him commit one blunder after another during the Battle of Britain. He failed to press home his attack on the radar stations and he was too willing to listen

German bomber crews eager for Adlertag *to get underway. They were brimming with confidence after their successes in Poland, Norway and France.*

to the extreme claims of his intelligence analysts about the success of the Luftwaffe missions. He failed to set the right targets for his bombers and he weakened the effectiveness of his fighters by tying them too closely to the slower bombers.

Now, at this crucial juncture, the Luftwaffe high command spent twenty four hours sipping wine with their leader. Whilst they were away, the weather improved and on the morning of 15th August a duty commander telephoned Karinhall for instructions now that the sky was clear and blue. Told that Goering and his commanders were not to be interrupted, the local officer gave the order to go ahead with the assault. By noon, the Luftwaffe attack had begun.

On this fine, sunny day, the Luftwaffe northern groups from Norway were the first to attack, heading this time for the Scottish coast and targets near Newcastle. Every squadron from Catterick to Drem near Edinburgh was scrambled. Out of range of the fighter escorts, the German bombers were badly done over by the fighters of 13 Group – 15 German bombers were shot down for the loss of one RAF fighter. Then more bombers, this time from Denmark, arrived over the Yorkshire coast. Leigh-Mallory scrambled squadrons from 12 Group. Seven Ju 88s were shot down. Later in the day, massive German raiding forces inflicted more serious damage on the airfields and the radar stations of the south-east. The raiders kept the RAF busy well into the evening. Despite the ground damage it had not been a good

Messerchmitt 110 crews plot their flight path.

day for the Luftwaffe – 71 aircraft had been lost against 29 for Fighter Command. And never again, would bombers without fighter escorts attack Britain from the northern bases. From now on the crucible of the Battle would be the south-east of England.

German intelligence continually underestimated the strength of RAF Fighter Command during the Battle of Britain. With the weakness common to most autocratic systems, the analysts never really wanted to report what their bosses did not want to hear. Before *Adlertag* they calculated that the RAF could not put more than 450 fighters into the air against them. In fact, with the increase in the replacement rate from the factories spurred into overdrive by Lord Beaverbrook at the Ministry of Aircraft Production, Dowding had about 750 fighters at his disposal. And the Luftwaffe were certain they had completely destroyed several fighter airfields, whereas in fact only Manston was effectively out of action. Intelligence as to targets was also poor. The Luftwaffe never clearly identified the key industrial sites they needed to destroy first of all to impact upon the Battle of Britain itself – like the factories where the Spitfires and Hurricanes were pouring off the production lines. But now Goering made another mistake. At his awayday at Karinhall, he ordered the Luftwaffe to discontinue their attacks on the radar stations as not one of them had been totally disabled. Had they persisted with their attacks on these radar stations, they would have blinded the RAF. It was a fatal error but would not

The crew of a Junkers 88A-1 are helped into their flying kit by their ground crew.

be Goering's last blunder.

Throughout August the two adversaries battled away. The Luftwaffe continued to suffer immense punishment – especially the dive bombing Stukas that had brought terror to the hearts of the men trying to get off the Dunkirk beaches only a few weeks earlier. The Ju 87s were no match for the Spitfire or the Hurricane and almost always came off worst in the daily dogfights over England. It was decided to phase them out of the Battle of Britain. On the other hand, the Bf 109s continued to perform well. Air Vice Marshall Park called on his pilots to avoid the fighter escorts and always go for the bombers. He knew that if the bombers endured heavier losses they would call on ever greater numbers of fighter escorts which would limit the number of sorties. Meanwhile, Goering in another tactical blunder called on his Bf 109 pilots to fly in ever closer formation with the bombers they were escorting – fatally restricting their room for manoeuvre. All fighter pilots try to exploit advantages of altitude and speed against the enemy. By tying the fighters closely to the bombers, Goering took away the advantage of both. But he wanted to give his bomber pilots the reassurance of being able to see their fighter escorts and know they were there.

The major problem facing the Bf 109 pilots came from the aircraft's weak wings. Potentially faster in a dive than the Spitfire, the 109 pilots had to pull out of the dive sooner into a relatively shallow curve in

A Heinkel III takes off with its bombload.

order to avoid the G-forces tearing the wings off. This made them vulnerable to the Spitfires who could catch up and fire at them as they flattened out. And although they were supposed to be able to turn more tightly than a Spitfire, in practice few pilots were willing to risk loosing their wings by pushing their aircraft to its limits. In the reality of day to day dogfights, the Spitfire was emerging as the superior fighter of the skies.

Another of the problems the Bf 109 pilots suffered from was the shortness of time they could spend over England. They could remain over English territory only for about 20 minutes before having to turn for home before their fuel ran out. And a slight miscalculation could mean having to bale out over the Channel or crash landing in Northern France. During August, the Bf 109 squadrons were re-positioned in airfields along the Pas de Calais to give them vital extra minutes over England. But, fortunately for the RAF, the Luftwaffe did not fit extra long-range fuel tanks on their Bf 109s. The technology existed to add an extra tank below the fuselage that would have given the Bf 109 another 20 minutes over England. But this was not done. Had this addition been made, it could have turned the course of the Battle of Britain.

A week after *Adlertag,* Luftwaffe intelligence again made estimates of the strength of Fighter Command – and again got it wrong. They now calculated that Dowding was down to about 300 operational

Pilot and observer in a Heinkel III keep watch for defending fighters.

fighters. In fact the figure was more like 700 available planes. Luftwaffe pilots increasingly began to be suspicious of their intelligence reports, as on each sortie they were attacked by more squadrons of Spitfires and Hurricanes. As they came under attack the Luftwaffe pilots would joke bitterly, right to the end of the Battle, that yet again they had found 'the last fifty Spitfires'.

Dowding's major problem by mid August was not the availability of planes, which were coming through in good numbers, it was the loss of trained pilots. A week after Eagle Day, Fighter Command had lost nearly 80% of its squadron commanders dead, wounded or resting from the strains of continuous combat. In August, Dowding agreed to reduce the Operational Training period to two weeks – it had been six months only a short while earlier. Pilots with only a few hours flying experience on the Spitfire or the Hurricane were now being thrown into the heat of battle. It was like a Formula One racing team handing over fast, highly developed vehicles to novice drivers. But this was war. There was little attempt by the RAF to pass on the skills learned by its veteran pilots to its rookie recruits. And this situation was no doubt exacerbated by the unwillingness of many experienced pilots to fly alongside novice airmen. They thought the novices would slow them down and cramp their style.

As the weather improved so the daily combats increased and the Battle of Britain entered its most desperate phase from 24th August.

Propaganda designed to reassure the British public during the months of extreme crisis can be seen in this Government booklet **The Battle of Britain***.*

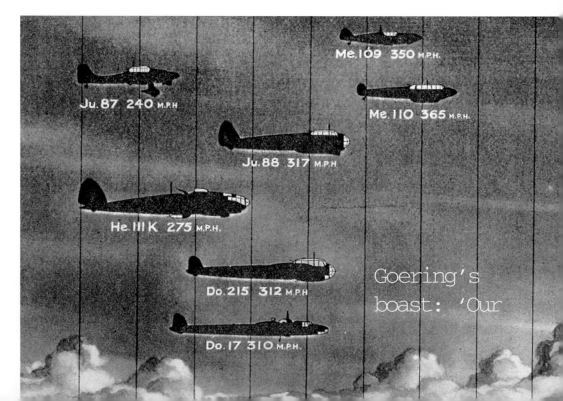

Me.109 350 M.P.H.

Ju.87 240 M.P.H

Me.110 365 M.P.H.

Ju.88 317 M.P.H

He.111 K 275 M.P.H.

Do.215 312 M.P.H

Goering's boast: 'Our

Do.17 310 M.P.H.

The Luftwaffe dispatched huge fleets of bombers to attack the RAF airfields and crucial industrial targets around the clock. There was to be no let up in the onslaught. Day after day Park tried to hold back his response to the arrival of another formation of German bombers, in case this proved to be a feint to draw out his fighters before an even bigger force appeared. On 26th August there were three major assaults during the day. 616 Squadron lost five out of its twelve planes in a battle between Canterbury and Maidstone at midday; in the afternoon another massed formation of bombers was intercepted over the Thames estuary and furious dogfights ensued in which the RAF came off best; and finally in the late afternoon, the Luftwaffe launched a major raid on Portsmouth. On the following day, RAF fighters found themselves up against a sweep consisting of only German fighters. The British pilots shot down six, for the loss of five of their own – but Park was furious, wanting his fighters to be deployed only against enemy bombers and not to be drawn into unproductive conflicts with fighters.

Within RAF Fighter Command the strains were now beginning to tell. On 26th August, Leigh-Mallory's 12 Group failed to come to the aid of Park's 11 Group when all its squadrons were mobilised. As a consequence, the 11 Group airfield at Debden in Essex was left undefended and was badly bombed. Park and Leigh-Mallory fell into dispute over the best tactics to defend Britain. Leigh-Mallory picked

The Spitfire is depicted as being faster than the German aircraft – albeit by just one mile an hour over the Messerschmitt 110. By contrast, the all-but forgotten Defiant is revealed to be slower than the German bombers!

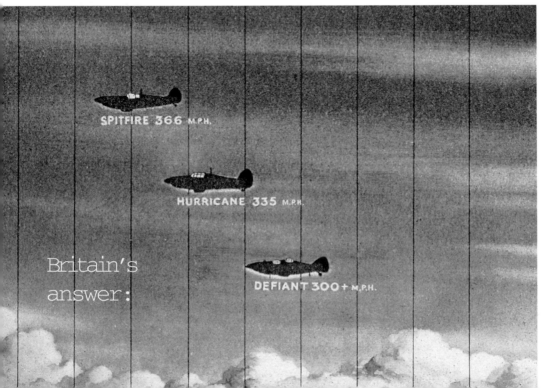

SPITFIRE 366 M.P.H.

HURRICANE 335 M.P.H.

Britain's answer:

DEFIANT 300+ M.P.H.

up the ideas of one of his squadron commanders who later received immortality as the hero of a feature film. Douglas Bader who had lost both his legs in a prewar flying accident whilst performing aerobatics, now commanded 242 Squadron at Duxford outside Cambridge. He argued that the most effective way to attack the German bombers was in mass formations consisting of three or more squadrons. These became known as 'big wings'. Bader believed that Dowding and Park dissipated the impact of the RAF by attacking only at squadron strength, keeping other squadrons standing by to respond to later assaults. Some of the 'big wing' theorists argued that it was better to wait and attack enemy bombers in force after they had dropped their bombs and were returning home in order to decimate the bombers, rather than cause lesser damage by minor assaults on their flanks as they approached their bomb run. And Bader was a great believer in the pilot being able to fight as he saw fit in the air, not under the command of controllers on the ground. Churchill met with Bader and he too became involved in the dispute.

This 'big wing controversy' as it became known, in part reflected the different circumstances of 11 and 12 Group. It took considerable time for several squadrons to rendezvous and form up – time that rarely existed during the attacks on 11 Group in the south-east, but which was available with the longer warning period enjoyed by 12 Group when it came under attack. And the 12 Group fighter pilots

The 'eyes' of the RAF during the Battle of Britain – radar stations situated along the south coast picked up the German bombers and fighters as they formed up over France, prior to their cross-Channel attack.

were frustrated at being on the fringes of the main Battle being fought out with 11 Group. The controversy rumbled on and caused ill feeling within the RAF. Without doubt it left slurs against the reputations of Dowding and Park after the Battle was over. And the growing feud between Park and Leigh-Mallory only weakened the effectiveness of the Fighter Command structure that Dowding had put in place before the war.

The Air Ministry's treatment of Dowding was nothing short of a scandal. Throughout the Battle of France and then the Battle of Britain, he laboured under the threat of retirement which was only reluctantly postponed on three occasions. This caused him intense personal distress. And the 'big wing controversy' with Leigh-Mallory left him unpopular, isolated and out-manoeuvred. In October 1940, instead of being congratulated for bringing the RAF successfully through the Battle of Britain he was unceremoniously removed from active service after an enquiry into air strategy. He was given 24 hours to vacate his office. The Americans love a winner and no doubt would have feted him as a national hero. But in Britain, Dowding never became a Nelson figure, celebrated for having saved the country from invasion. However, without doubt, Dowding's work in the four years from 1936-40 laid the foundation on which the RAF were able to survive the Battle of Britain and to continue to fight another day.

While the senior players in RAF Fighter Command fought their

The incoming aerial armadas are plotted in the Operations Rooms of RAF Fighter Stations. Time to get the boys up to tackle the 'Bandits'!

own internal battles, life on a Spitfire squadron fell into a steady and relentless routine. For most of the day, the pilots remained in a state of waiting. They would sleep or play cards or chess; the calmer ones would try to read, often magazines rather than books. At some stations, someone would bring out a gramophone and the pilots would doze listening to the hits of the day. Many pilots remember the strain of this constant waiting as the most draining experience of the Battle. When the telephone rang there would be instant tension. Sometimes it was only to announce that the NAAFI were coming around with tea. At other times the order to scramble would be barked out. The pilots would drop everything and race to their planes. The groundcrew might get the engine started. The pilots would leap in and strap up and get going, taking off across the grass in a desperate rush to get airborne and to gain height. Literally every second counted. In their haste, pilots occasionally forgot to buckle up their parachutes which caused tragedy on the few occasions when they needed to bail out.

With ammunition for only about fifteen seconds of firing, the planes would often come back to base to reload and then take off again and return to the fray. Sometimes a pilot would fly as many as five sorties in a day. The strain was immense. Despite the long, stressful days, pilots would still go out to the local pub when they could of an evening. 'It was our only time to do a bit of living' remembered Denis

Pilots awaiting the call to scramble. Many found the long hours of standby more stressful than actual combat.

RAF JARGON

Kite –	aircraft
Scramble –	take off immediately
Vector –	steer a course
Buster –	fly at all speed
Orbit –	maintain a position
Pancake –	land
Angels –	height, given in thousands of feet, eg Angels One Five – 15,000 feet
Bogey –	an unidentified aircraft
Bandit –	an enemy aircraft
Tally-ho –	the command to attack
Ditch –	a landing in the sea
Prang –	a crash, eg Wizard Prang – a spectacular crash
Kill –	an enemy aircraft shot down

Robinson later. But 'Bam' Bamberger recalls that he no longer felt comfortable outside the narrow world of the fighter station. It was impossible to explain to outsiders what the pilots were going through. They would often drink too much and return to base late – only to be standing by for action a few hours later at dawn.

The groundcrew played a vital but often overlooked role in the Battle of Britain. Seven days a week the crews were up at dawn for engine runs and inspections. When an aircraft returned from a sortie and taxied to its parking bay it was instantly surrounded by the small army that made up a groundcrew team. The plane had to be refuelled as quickly as possible. Armourers had to rearm the eight machine guns, each one fed by a belt of three hundred .303 bullets. Mechanics would inspect any damage and make decisions about repairs in an instant. Bullet holes were patched over. Engines had to be serviced – or at times simply removed and replaced which proved quicker. With spare parts at a premium all sorts of solutions had to be improvised to keep a plane combat-worthy. No groundcrew ever wanted to see their aircraft out of the battle.

The camaraderie built up between a pilot and his groundcrew was intense. Every pilot was totally reliant upon the skill and dedication of his crew. The groundcrews were intensely protective of their pilot and plane and were filled with pride when he came back and reported a 'kill'. They learned to understand their plane's character and

Scramble! Pilots of a Hurricane Squadron race to their machines.

personality, which they had to struggle with in order to keep it operational. And it was not only the pilots who experienced danger. With the airfields increasingly becoming Luftwaffe targets, more and more of the groundstaff found themselves in the firing line and casualties at some airfields were considerable. Something else that pilots and groundcrew shared was the tiredness that overwhelmed them whenever a job had been completed. Across every Battle of Britain airfield, exhausted pilots, armourers, riggers and mechanics were to be seen sleeping on the grass whenever an opportunity arose.

Another extraordinary feature of the Battle of Britain was that it was taking place in full view of the people of south-east England. Every day workers, housewives and school kids could hear the roar of the fighters and look up to see the vapour trails in the sky above them as the two sides locked in aerial combat. Occasionally the grandstand view would be interrupted as an aircraft came plummeting downwards in flames. The local policeman or Home Guard would race to the scene to arrest the pilot and guard the wreckage until scientists from the Air Ministry had come to examine the damage and remove vital parts. Often, these local officials were over keen and

Groundcrew swarm over this Spitfire readying it for take-off. Each pilot was totally reliant upon the skills of his fitters, armourers, riggers and electricians, who rarely let him down.

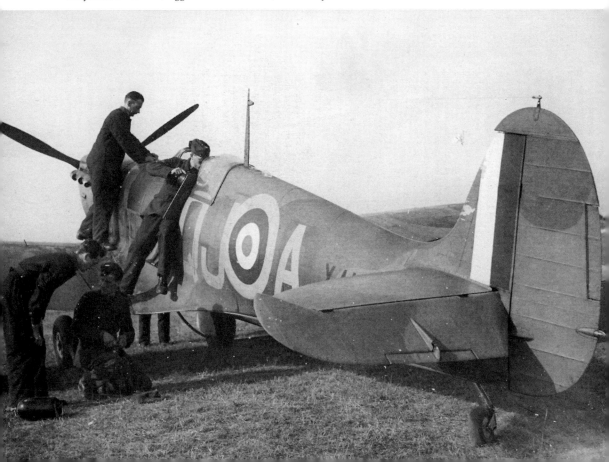

failed to distinguish between Allied airmen and Germans to be captured.

Squadron Leader James Nicholson, the only fighter pilot to win a VC in the war, baled out of his plane badly burned on the face and hands, but when he landed was fired on by a trigger happy member of the Home Guard. In September the government had to announce that not every parachutist was an enemy. For schoolboys there was unique caché in recovering pieces of a downed aircraft – just as there was later in finding pieces of still-hot shrapnel in blitzed buildings. But for now, the RAF fighter pilots became romantic heroes, bravely fighting in one-to-one type gladiatorial combats, to defend the homeland from a vicious and numerically superior foe. Many of the myths surrounding the Battle of Britain grew up at this time in what became known as 'Spitfire Summer'.

The Spitfire's classic outline made it popular with the public. Spitfire Funds were established across Britain in the summer of 1940 to raise money to 'buy' an aircraft. The price was £5000 and before long almost every city had collected money and had its name on a Spitfire. The hat was passed around in factories and schools and even amongst

This Spitfire pilot will be in the air in less than a minute – the engine of his 'kite' is already ticking over.

unemployed miners. About a million pounds were collected each month. The legend of the Spitfire was growing daily.

By early September, the Battle of Britain had entered its most crucial phase. On several days three separate waves of German bombers and fighters would come in the morning, afternoon and early evening. And as the experienced pilots were replaced by the novice airmen, it seemed that the tables were slowly turning against the RAF. Biggin Hill airfield was hit badly and the Sector Operations Room was put out of action. On 1st September, Bf 109s and Bf 110s caught 54 Squadron as they climbed to intercept and with the crucial advantage of altitude the German fighters shot down five Spitfires. Out of eighteen pilots in 85 Squadron, fourteen were shot down during this period, including Squadron Leader Peter Townsend. Two of the pilots were shot down twice. Few units could sustain this level of losses and survive as an effective fighting force. 85 Squadron, along with several others, was withdrawn from the Battle to rest up. Park continued to insist that his fighters must avoid the German fighters whenever possible and should only engage with the enemy's bombers.

In a series of dogfights on 3rd September, the RAF and the Luftwaffe both lost sixteen aircraft each. And two days later, the RAF lost twenty-two aircraft shot down whilst the Luftwaffe suffered twenty-one losses. In addition, the Germans had finally turned their attention towards the vital aircraft production factories and were

A Spitfire pilot ready to meet the enemy. Note the rear-view mirror mounted above the hood.

hitting their new targets with deadly accuracy – the Vickers Wellington factory was put out action for days after a series of direct hits resulted in nearly 100 deaths and 600 casualties. Again, a mixture of good luck and bad intelligence by the Luftwaffe meant that most of the essential Spitfire and Hurricane factories remained in production. But in a two week period Dowding had lost 25% of his pilots and a quarter of his fighter squadrons were made up of pilots with less than two weeks flying experience. Overall it seemed that RAF Fighter Command was losing the Battle of Britain.

Hitler had instructed the Luftwaffe not to carry out terror bombing raids against British cities. But on the night of 24th August a small group of German Heinkel He 111s became separated from their squadron which was on a mission to bomb oil storage depots in the Midlands. Whether they panicked or just got lost and thought they were over the target is not known but they dropped their bombs on the suburbs of London in defiance of orders. Nine civilians were killed. Churchill immediately ordered Bomber Command to retaliate by bombing Berlin. On the following night, a force of 80 Wellington bombers raided the German capital. Three days later the RAF bombed Berlin again. This time German civilians were killed. Berliners were angry. Goering, who had said that Allied bombers would never fly over the Reich, was deeply embarrassed. After a third raid Hitler became furious and lifted the ban on the bombing of British cities. He

Chocks away! This Spitfire is being turned into the wind, assisted by its groundcrew, prior to take-off.

provoked hysterical applause when he announced to a small gathering that Britain's cities would be 'razed to the ground' in reprisal. Meanwhile, in conference with his commanders at The Hague, Goering decided that the continuous assault against the RAF was not succeeding and a change of tactics was called for.

In the late afternoon of Saturday 7th September, British radar picked up what appeared to be the biggest force of bombers yet, heading towards the Kent coast at Deal. Indeed there were nearly 1,000 aircraft, one third of which were bombers. This vast attacking force formed a black cloud covering nearly 800 square miles of airspace. Goering himself had taken his personal train up to the Pas de Calais to see the force fly off. At Fighter Command HQ in Bentley Priory, the controllers interpreted the appearance of this immense force as signs of another attack on the sector airfields to the north of London. Park ordered his fighters to stay north and wait. The huge mass of German bombers crossed the Channel and the telephone lines crackled as countless Observers across south east England phoned in their reports. But the German bombers flew on across the advanced sector airfields, across the sprawling suburbs to the south east of London and instead homed in on a new target – the vast docks and factories to the east of London. After the first wave of bombers dropped their bombs and incendiaries, a second wave flew in and guided by the flames poured their explosives into the cauldron below. It was only after the worst of

In the race to get airborne the fighter pilots of a squadron would spread out across its grass airfield and take off together.

the bombing was over that the controllers at Bentley Priory realised that the main assault of the day was not against the RAF airfields but against the city and people of London.

This shift of tactics caused terrible mayhem on the ground. The docks provided the lifeblood for London. They were the heart of a great trading empire. In London's Surrey Docks, the German bombs set ablaze 250 acres of timber. Warehouses of paint, rum, rubber, flour and paper burst into flames. Thousands of firefighters from across southern England rushed to the scene and struggled to contain the huge fires. They battled the flames throughout the night. In the densely packed streets of the East End where most of the dockers lived who kept the goods flowing in and out of Britain, 448 civilians were killed and hundreds more injured. Whole districts were cut off and surrounded by flames. One fire officer called for reinforcements with the now famous words 'Send all the pumps you've got; the whole bloody world's on fire.'

That evening, the Chiefs of Staff met with Churchill in the underground bunker known now as the Cabinet War Rooms, within sound of the falling bombs on the East End. They were considering the build up of landing barges along the French coast. Reports came in of the arrest of some Germans in a rowing boat off the Kent coast. Just after 8.00 pm as the raid was at its height, the Chiefs issued the codeword 'Cromwell'. This was the warning to army commanders

A tight formation of Heinkel IIIs heading for targets in the south of England.

that invasion was imminent. Some local Home Guard officials also received the codeword but mistook it for news that the invasion had actually taken place. In some villages the church bells were rung which was a signal that German parachutists were landing. In this tense and heightened atmosphere, this overreaction later caused great embarrassment. Fortunately there was no widespread panic. But across Britain, people realised the Battle of Britain was reaching its climax.

Over the next few days the Luftwaffe kept up its aerial onslaught against London. Waves of bombers flew over the city by day followed by more bombers at night. 412 civilians were killed on Sunday 8th, a further 370 on 9th. The RAF pilots were putting up stiff resistance but outnumbered in the air, they were often outfought and outgunned. On 11th September, the RAF lost 31 fighters to 22 aircraft of the Luftwaffe. And the bombs rained down on the docks, on the East End and right across London as far as the West End and Kensington. The Luftwaffe were convinced that this would soon destroy the spirit of the British people and force them to sue for peace, in a way that their constant battering of the RAF had failed to achieve. But for the RAF, Goering's change of tactic was a blessed relief. It was down to reserves of 80 Hurricanes and 47 Spitfires. With the pressure off the airfields, Fighter Command could begin to take stock and reassemble its forces.

The climax of the Battle of Britain was now only a few days away.

Left: *The cramped and busy cockpit of a twin-engined Bf110. This type was designed as a fighter, but before the Battle of Britain was over it had to have fighter protection itself from the Hurricanes and Spitfires. It was relegated to fighter-bomber and night fighter roles.*

Right: *This German gunner's single weapon gave little protection against the eight machine guns of an attacking Spitfire.*

On Sunday 15th September, the Luftwaffe attacked in two large waves in the morning and the afternoon. Park's fighters just had enough time to refuel and rearm in between. The groundcrews worked like heroes to get their planes airborne again. And this time, Bader's 'big wing' flying in from the north gave the German bombers a heavy mauling. But the RAF could not carry on like this for much longer. The Prime Minister chose this of all days to drive from his weekend retreat, Chequers, across to Park's 11 Group headquarters at Uxbridge. There he anxiously followed the battle as WAAFs moved the counters across the board map of southern England. Signals came in reporting '40 plus' raiders, then '60 plus', then '80 plus'. Eventually, all the squadrons were ordered into the air. Three reserve squadrons were called in from neighbouring 12 Group. On the blackboards around the walls there were no other squadrons listed as standing by. Churchill went over and spoke to Park who looked tense. Churchill asked 'What other reserves have we?' The chilling reply came back 'There are none.' Churchill looked grave. Both men realised that the game was nearly up. One further wave of German bombers and the airfields, the city of London, indeed the very survival of Britain would be at stake. But no more bombers came. Goering had pushed the Luftwaffe to its limit.

At their bases that evening the German commanders, who believed the RAF had been blown out of the sky, were amazed to hear of the big wing attack when more fighters than ever before had swept down on their bombers. And the Luftwaffe came out of the day by far the worse off. The RAF reported that it had shot down 185 German aircraft. The

true number, revealed after the war, was fifty-six German losses against twenty-seven RAF fighters. But this was enough. The Luftwaffe could endure such losses no longer. The weather was changing and autumn was setting in. The moment for a seaborne invasion had passed. Two days later, realising that he had failed to win command of the skies, Hitler issued a secret order postponing Operation Sealion. Over the next few weeks he would begin preparing

'Achtung Spitfire!'

for his invasion of the Soviet Union. The plan to invade Britain would be postponed indefinitely.

Daytime raids on airfields and cities continued into October, but it is clear that 15th September was a turning point. It is this day that is still remembered as 'Battle of Britain Day' across the UK. By now, the Luftwaffe too was exhausted and demoralised. Constantly being told that the RAF were on their last legs, the bomber and fighter crews despaired as more and more Spitfires and Hurricanes came at them. Still, in most fighter versus fighter dogfights both sides came off about the same. But whenever the British fighters tore into the slow moving bombers they caused major damage. Although both sides maintained a level of chivalry throughout the Battle, the Luftwaffe had given up on its titanic struggle with the RAF. They preferred to bomb by night when the fighters had less chance of finding them. And flying above 15,000 feet, the anti-aircraft guns and the searchlights were unlikely to get them. German

A 'kill'. The death of a Bf110 caught by the gun-camera of a British fighter.

bomber losses declined rapidly.

Throughout the autumn and into the winter, the Luftwaffe mercilessly carried out its blitz against London and other cities of Britain. London was blitzed with only one night's respite, for seventy-six consecutive nights. The routine for millions of Londoners involved taking to deep shelters like the Tube stations at night and clearing up and carrying on with 'Business as Usual' as best as they could by day. Other cities like Portsmouth, Bristol, Plymouth, Birmingham and Liverpool were all heavily bombed. In the worst bombing raid of all, on the town of Coventry on the night of 14th November, 554 civilians were killed in a single raid. There were so many corpses they were lined up and given a mass burial. A hundred acres of the medieval city centre was destroyed and about one third of the city's houses were made uninhabitable. Mostly morale stood up to the onslaught, although on some occasions there was panic and severe social breakdown followed the bombing raids on Southampton. But British society did not crumble. The production of weapons and munitions continued, and the government did not seek a peace settlement with Germany.

There have been many disputes and different interpretations of the Battle of Britain. There have been arguments about the numbers of German and RAF planes shot down; disagreements as to whether Hitler ever seriously intended to invade Britain or not; controversy

A soldier stands guard over this wrecked Dornier 17Z-2 brought down during the air fighting over the south of England. It has already had the swastika chopped from the tail fin by a souvenir hunter.

over tactics and strategy on both sides and ultimately differences of opinion as to who won and who lost the Battle. All of these are important issues. But more than anything else, one overriding fact is clear. Having conquered most of northern Europe, it was inevitable that Nazi Germany would turn its attention against the British Isles. In the Battle of Britain, Hitler had to win mastery of the skies if he was to launch an invasion with any chance of success, or force the British government to admit that it was hopeless to fight on. In neither of these objectives did Goering's Luftwaffe succeed. By surviving to fight another day, the RAF ensured that Britain would be able to hit back at Nazi Germany later. This it did tenfold. The entire tonnage of bombs dropped on London throughout the winter of 1940-41 was equivalent to only a single week's worth of bombs dropped on Germany, later in the war. And, of course, when the United States entered the war, Britain became the armed camp from which the ultimately successful invasion and re-conquest of Europe could take place. It is inconceivable that D-Day could have been launched from the other side of the Atlantic.

The RAF might not have won the Battle of Britain in a traditional way by defeating its enemy outright. But in not loosing it, Britain had won the most important victory of all. Hitler turned his attention to the Soviet Union and his plans for mastery in the East. But his fatal blunder was in not defeating Britain in the summer of 1940. In the

Spitfires returning to Base. Now they must re-arm and re-fuel before the next scramble is ordered.

course of the Second World War, the Battle of Britain was a decisive turning point. Along with the Hurricane, the machine that had done more than anything else to ensure Britain's survival was the Spitfire. Brilliantly designed by Reginald Mitchell, magnificently flown and kept in the skies by hundreds of pilots, groundcrews, planners, radar operators and observers, the Spitfire had won its spurs as one of the great fighting machines of history. And as Churchill movingly put it, 'Never in the field of human conflict has so much been owed by so many to so few.'

For the Spitfire, the Battle of Britain was only the beginning. Joe Smith's view that the design should be developed rather than replaced, was proved right. Spitfires were armed with cannon for ground attack missions, they were fitted with racks to carry bombs and rockets and a maritime version, the Seafire, was designed with folding wings, for use on aircraft carriers. When Spitfire production finally ended in 1949, more than 22,000 machines had been produced – not bad for a design which came close to being strangled in its infancy by official 'red tape'.

It's hard to say whether the final Spitfire, the Mark 24, was in any sense the same aircraft which had fought the Battle of Britain. It kept the name, but its engine was twice as powerful, it weighed about a ton and a half more, and was 100 mph faster. It had changed from a finely balanced rapier – described by one over-confident German pilot as a

These classic Battle of Britain Spitfires (MkIIB), are a far cry from the MkXIV below, with its five-bladed propeller, tear-drop canopy, low rear fuselage and large tail fin.

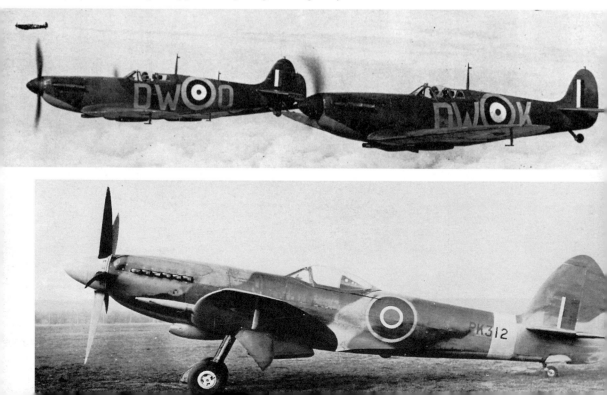

'pretty little toy' – into a fearsome broadsword. Its armour-piercing cannon could demolish a locomotive, or slice the wing off an aircraft in a split-second. The big engine and big guns were revealed by tell-tale bulges in the sleek outline. A tear-drop canopy and low back, gave it an entirely different shape. Its huge, five-bladed propeller was efficient, but ungainly, and required an equally oversized tail fin and rudder, to counteract its torque. But, through most of the changes, Mitchell's wing design survived, very much as he had conceived it in the mid 1930s. Many Spitfires lost their pointed wing tips, but the 'clipped' wing still retained the original's structure – if not its purity of line. Only in the final versions, were the last vestiges of Mitchell's original design replaced. The Spitfire became like the woodman's favourite axe – six new handles and two new blades, but still the best axe he'd ever had. The machine changed beyond recognition, but the name survived because nobody wanted to say goodbye to the Spitfire. It represented Britain's finest hour and, at a critical moment in history, it had proved to be the best tool for a tough job.

The Spitfire finally passed into history with the coming of the Jet Age. But not before a MkXIV managed to become the first RAF fighter to shoot down a German Me 262 jet in combat. The RAF flew its last operational Spitfire mission on 1st April 1954 and the type was officially withdrawn from service in 1957. The delta-winged, supersonic fighters that replaced the Spitfire, owed much of their

Spitfire PR Mark XIX, PM 631, belonging to the Battle of Britain Memorial Flight. This particular aircraft was built too late to see service in the war being delivered to the RAF in November 1945.

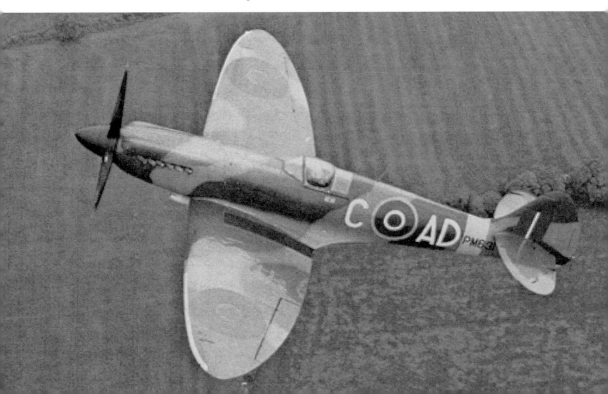

success to the work of Reginald Mitchell. His vision of the future produced an airframe in 1936, that would not look unfamiliar to a present-day aircraft engineer. The brave young Spitfire pilots who fought and won the Battle of Britain have rightly earned their place in the Nation's Roll of Honour. But other names should not be forgotten: Lady Houston, who financed the S.6B, test pilots Jeffrey Quill and Alex Henshaw, Joe Smith who kept the project alive after the death of its creator – and Reginald Mitchell – Aircraft Designer Extraordinary.

VINTAGE SPITS

Today, there are thought to be about 200 Surviving Spitfires worldwide – roughly one per cent of the total built. Some are carefully preserved in museums, some are exposed to the elements, suffering from corrosion and neglect, some are little more than piles of scrap metal. But about a quarter of them have been restored to flying condition. The Spitfire can still stir the emotions like few other machines and as long as there are multi-millionaires who dream of flying their own Spitfire, and skilled engineers who understand its very special qualities, the Spitfire will fly on.

In Britain, the small, grass airfield at Audley End, north east of London, regularly echoes to the sound of a Spitfire. It is the home of Historic Flying Ltd, a company whose business is rebuilding Spitfires. Here, using traditional skills and materials, they regularly transform long-grounded hulks into living, breathing aircraft, as good as the day they left the factory. It's a painstaking and labour-intensive process. Each rebuild can take more than 10,000 man-hours – a full year's work for four people. It's a far cry from the days when thousands were employed, producing dozens of aircraft every week. But the same skills and the same processes are still involved. There are no short-cuts to restoring a Spitfire and all the problems that made its mass-production such a fraught process in wartime, now confront a new generation.

As today's engineers dismantle and re-assemble the Spitfire's airframe and its engine, they become almost like archeologists digging into the past. To understand the machine fully, they have to immerse themselves in its history, entering the world of wartime production: a world of long hours toiling at the workbench, of rationing, of blackout regulations. Today at least, they can work without the constant threat of air raids and the endless pressure to turn out aircraft, at a time when Britain was fighting for its very survival and depending on the Spitfire to be its saviour.

Chapter Three

THE DC-3 STORY

Of all the classic aircraft designs, the DC-3 is generally accepted as the one which has created the most impact on people's lives, in war and in peace. The word 'Classic' once defined the great works of literature, art and architecture of the past. It meant culture: Greek temples and Roman statues, the works of Shakespeare and the Mona Lisa, but it firmly ignored industry. Now the word is regularly applied to industrial design and awarded to manufactured objects which are merely old and anything but classics: a badly built car from the 1950s, an inefficient 1940s radio, anything made in the 1930s. But, at its best, the word gives long overdue status to the great achievements of the industrial revolution that fall outside the academic world and sometimes the word fits like a glove.

The qualities of a classic are elusive – a subtle combination of performance and appearance. Shape is crucial: while one shape says 'car', a few changes can make it no more than a box on wheels. Modern ships can look more like floating housing developments, but there's no confusing the outline of the 'Titanic'. British road signs at

The classic design of the DC-3 lent itself to tasteful livery adornment, as seen on this United Air Lines example delivered new in 1940. The highly polished metal skin and the streamlined shape created an impression of speed and style.

open railway crossings still show the outline of a steam locomotive, its the shape that says 'train', even to a generation that never knew steam. Ask a child to draw an aeroplane and there is a good chance that it will produce a version of a shape that began life in the 1930s – the Douglas DC-3 airliner which, by any reckoning, has to be counted a Classic. During a long and distinguished career, it has collected a confusing series of names and numbers. In military service the DC-3 became the C-47. To the British it was the 'Dakota', while Americans often called it the 'Skytrain', or the 'Gooney'. But there is no confusion about its place in the history of aviation. It is, after all, the most important single aircraft design ever built.

When the Wright Brothers launched the age of powered flight on December 17th 1903, they began a revolution as profound as any yet seen. If the 19th Century was the age of steam and the industrial revolution, the 20th was the age of internal combustion and mass transport. In the new Millennium as the world-wide electronic revolution gathers pace, it's easy to forget how little people knew of the world before mass air travel opened it up. The lone pioneers like Bleriot and Lindbergh proved it could be done, but it was the DC-3 of 1935 which actually did it. And it still does. Hundreds of DC-3s are still in service and, as the type enters the 21st Century, it has been airborne for more than two thirds of the entire history of powered flight.

Will it fly? Boulton and Paul's 'Bodmin' aircraft of 1922. Its two engines were contained within the fuselage and the power was transmitted to the propellers through gears and drive shafts.

The early years of the flying revolution were full of triumph and disaster. Aircraft were fragile and dangerous machines. Until engines could be produced which combined high power with minimum weight, aircraft had to be as light as possible, which meant a wire-braced wooden frame, covered with fabric. By the late 1920s, passenger airlines had been established in many countries. The pioneer days of flight now have an aura of glamour, but the biplane aircraft were slow and very noisy, with cramped and unheated cabins. The few intrepid passengers would be tossed about by the slightest turbulence and

Despite its defeat in the Great War and restrictions imposed by the Treaty of Versailles, Germany managed to establish a civil airline – **Luft Hansa.** *There was no shortage of pilots and modified bomber aircraft. Here a well-to-do passenger climbs aboard a fragile looking Fokker FII.*

The Handley Page Imperial Airways 'liner' the HP.42 of the early 1930s was the first of the four-engined airliners. This strutted biplane with a top speed of 120 miles per hour was already outdated by the time it entered service.

air-sickness was always a problem. There were superficial touches of lightweight luxury, designed to create the ambience of a railway Pullman car: curtains, wicker armchairs, linen tablecloths – but in reality, passenger planes were more like a cross between a garden shed and a tent. The combination of discomfort and high cost meant that few people chose (or could afford) to fly, and the airlines depended on government mail carrying contracts for most of their income.

As the 1930s began, the only real signs of progress were a gradual move to monoplanes, mostly fitted with three engines, and replacement of the fabric cover with sheet metal cladding. But the aircraft's strength still depended on a frame, made of wood or metal tubes, which produced an angular and boxy fuselage. Safety was also a constant problem. Since they were not pressurised, heated, or fitted with oxygen, passenger planes could not fly high enough to avoid the worst of the weather, or high mountain peaks and there were frequent accidents. On 31 March 1931, at Bazaar, Kansas, a wood-framed Fokker FXA belonging to Transcontinental and Western Airlines (TWA), broke up in mid air and crashed, killing all on board. An inspection of the wreckage revealed that plywood in the wing structure had de-laminated and split into layers. There was a public outcry, largely because a national football celebrity had died in the accident. The American government introduced strict new regulations for wood framed aircraft and the airlines were soon demanding a new

A classic of its day, the Ford 4/AT-B Tri-Motor. Its type represented a small step forward, having a single high positioned wing and metal cladding.

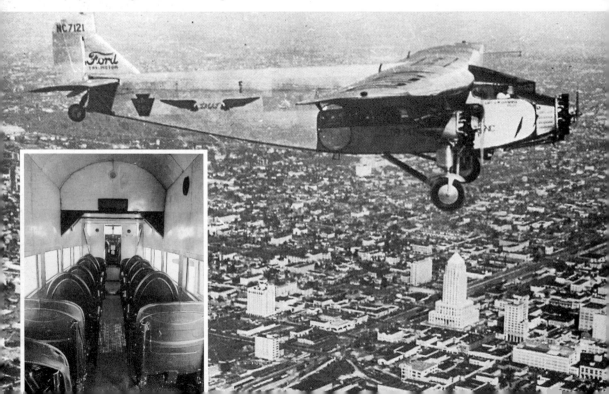

Another tri-motor design of the 1930s that found favour with the world's airlines and their passengers, because of its comfort and reliability, was the Junkers JU52, carrying up to eighteen people.

generation of better and safer machines from the aircraft builders.

The first company to successfully meet the challenge was Boeing. In 1933, they introduced the revolutionary 247. It was a streamlined, all-metal monoplane, with twin engines and a retracting undercarriage. Hailed as the first modern, 'airliner', it was fast and luxurious, but with only ten passenger seats, it was more like a flying limousine than an airliner. It also had some major drawbacks: the cabin was too low for tall passengers to stand upright, the main wing spar ran crossways through it and much of the interior space was occupied by the fuel tanks. But the sleek new plane was an instant hit with the public and every airline wanted to fly it.

Boeing had financial links with United Airlines, who promptly took over the entire production run with an order for sixty aircraft. The other airlines were told to place their orders and join the queue. But TWA were in no mood to wait. The Fokker crash had damaged their reputation and their business, they urgently needed to re-equip their fleet if they were to survive.

On 2 August 1932, TWA wrote to the leading American aircraft manufacturers (with the exception of Boeing), asking them to submit designs for a new aircraft. The brief was surprisingly cautious, given the clear lead set by Boeing.

'Type: All metal trimotor monoplane preferred but combination structure or biplane would be considered. Main internal structure must

A tremendous leap forward – the Boeing 247 transport, introduced in 1933. This ground-breaking machine began a revolution in aircraft design. It was the forerunner of the low-wing monoplane of the present-day.

be metal.'

This specification would have fitted an already obsolete aircraft like the Ford Trimotor of 1925! The fact that TWA didn't even specify that the new machine should be all-metal, shows how slow the industry was to realise the way in which aircraft design was evolving. They requested only twelve passenger seats – even the Ford had fourteen – and an ability to fly at up to 10,000 ft. The only really demanding clause required the ability to take off, fully loaded, from any of the airfields the company served with one engine out of action.

A copy of the letter landed on the desk of Donald W. Douglas, Chairman and founder of the Douglas Aircraft Company. He had established an aircraft factory in an old motion picture studio in Santa Monica, California in the 1920s and built up a reputation for producing successful, if unspectacular, civil and military biplanes. But he was about to transform the aircraft industry, and his own fortunes, by creating the most successful single aircraft design ever. Douglas later called the TWA letter 'the Birth Certificate of the Modern Airliner'.

After consulting his designers, Douglas responded less than two weeks later with an extraordinarily bold and advanced design. It was an all-metal monoplane, with swept wings and a large, unobstructed cabin, yet fitted with only two engines. This would mean taking off with only one, if the specification was to be met. TWA's technical

Donald W. Douglas Jr, founder of the Douglas Aircraft Company, was quick to see the possibilities of the low-wing monoplane.

TRANSCONTINENTAL & WESTERN AIR INC
100 CHARDS ROAD
MUNICIPAL AIRPORT
KANSAS CITY MISSOURI

August 2nd,
19 32

Douglas Aircraft Corporation,
Clover Field,
Santa Monica, California

Attention: Mr. Donald Douglas

Dear Mr. Douglas,

Transcontinental & Western Air is interested in purchasing ten or more trimotored transport planes. I am attaching our general performance specifications, covering this equipment and would appreciate your advising whether your company is interested in this manufacturing job.

If so, approximately how long would it take to turn out the first plane for service tests?

Very truly yours,

Jack Frye
Vice President
In Charge of Operations

JF/GS
Encl.

N.B. Please consider this information confidential and return specifications if you are not interested.

SAVE TIME - USE THE AIR MAIL

advisor was the celebrated hero of the first solo Transatlantic flight – Charles Lindbergh. He had doubts about the twin engine design, but TWA decided to place an order for a single prototype. In the drawing office, Donald Douglas hung up a cut-away diagram of the rival Boeing 247. He told his designers 'don't copy it: improve on it' – and they did.

On 1 July 1933, the Douglas Commercial, or DC-1, lifted off the runway for the first time. After initial problems with the engines, it began its test flying programme and soon proved its ability to match or exceed the TWA brief in every respect. It flew faster and higher than required and convinced Lindbergh and TWA that its two engines were sufficient by taking off with only one, then catching up with – and overtaking, a tri-motor using all three. The all-metal DC-1 was far stronger than the traditional designs. Rather than simply screwing metal panels onto a wire-braced, wooden frame, it used the tensile strength of the aluminum skin itself, to brace the structure and spread the wing loading evenly.

The DC-1 was much larger than the Boeing. Its spacious cabin had plenty of room for the twelve passengers, plus a host of

Right: *Inside the DC-1 with its two rows of six seats.*

Left: *First page of the letter which Donald Douglas called 'the Birth Certificate of the Modern Airliner'.*

Below: *The DC-1 prototype at Clover Field, California, about to set off on its maiden flight. Problems with the Wright SGR-1828-F engines caused the first flight to end early, but not before the those in attendance had been suitably impressed.*

refinements, including the first lavatory and washbasin ever installed on a passenger plane, a galley, generous sound proofing and cabin heating. TWA were delighted with the Douglas design. After various modifications it began setting a string of new speed and distance records, including a coast-to-coast flight of 3,107 miles, in just over eleven hours, at an average speed of 272 mph – faster than the American front line fighters then in service!

Fitted with two extra seats, the Douglas entered passenger service in 1934 as the DC-2 and soon became a best-seller. It instantly cut half an hour off the New York – Chicago schedule flown by United Airlines, with their Boeing 247s. Soon TWA were also offering regular and frequent DC-2 flights between New York and Los Angeles. But, with only fourteen seats per aircraft, fares remained high and profits still depended on flying the U.S. Mail as well. Following TWA's lead, other airlines began switching to the DC-2 and the War Department was soon among the satisfied customers of Donald Douglas. Their obsolete Fokker C-10s and Ford tri-motor transports were no match for the new DC-2. A military version was soon in production, known as the C-33. With a strengthened floor and a wide loading door on the left hand side, it could carry just over a ton of cargo, or twelve combat troops. Few could have guessed in 1934 how big a part this role would play in the story of the Douglas Transport ten years later.

The DC-2 looked like a triumph for Douglas, but the real

The two rivals seen here together, the Boeing and the Douglas airliners.

breakthrough was still to come. Commercial operators soon realised that the DC-2 design had scope for expansion. American Airlines, another rival to TWA, wanted to create a flying version of the Pullman Railway Car, fitted with sleeping berths for long-haul night flights. They also wanted the option of more passenger seats as well and longer range. Their engineers believed that the result could be achieved by retaining some 85% of the existing DC-2.

Donald Douglas was always inclined to caution and was not convinced that there was any need to change his highly successful design. He had invested huge sums in the project, now he wanted to sit back and make some much-needed profit. But Cyrus Smith, the dynamic president of American Airlines would not be put off. By the end of an historic, two-hour telephone call, he had promised Douglas a firm order for twenty enlarged DC-2 aircraft as well as agreeing to bear all the initial development costs. The offer was too good for Douglas to refuse. Both men respected each other and both drove a hard bargain. In many ways they were typical of the energetic, self-made businessmen who were gradually pulling America out of the Great Depression. It says much for their business methods that a verbal agreement was accepted as sufficient, no formal letter sealed a deal worth $4.5 million!

Donald Douglas proved that he was as good as his word by assigning 400 of his draftsmen and engineers to the task of enlarging

Wherever it went the new Douglas design drew crowds of admirers.

the DC-2. Working under Chief Engineer Arthur Raymond, the team set about re-assessing the DC-2. The obvious start was to round out the straight sides of the fuselage into an almost circular cross section. This created an extra 26 inches of width – enough to accommodate two rows of sleeping berths – which could be converted to 14 day seats, or three rows of fixed seats, giving a total of 21. The fuselage was also extended by more than two feet, while the wings were strengthened and their span was increased by ten feet, to include a longer and more graceful taper to the wing tip. The engines were up-rated to 1,000 hp. Initially, it was hoped that the work could be finished within a year. But, as more and more detailed improvements were added, it expanded to two years. Meanwhile American Airlines were not prospering and in 1935, they lost $748,000. They could only hope that the new plane would be worth waiting for.

What was actually taking place at the Douglas plant was another, if less dramatic, revolution. The all-metal aircraft had become established. Now it was evolving into a far more sophisticated machine. Wind tunnel tests and full-scale mock-ups of the cabin interior were helping to create the airliner of the future. Designers were given the task of creating an interior colour scheme which would help to encourage a mood of confidence among the passengers: dark for the floor, light for the ceiling. There were the small refinements: an electric shaver socket for the passengers, an electric cigarette lighter for

This Dutch owned DC-2, came second in the MacRobertson air race from England to Australia in 1934. Averaging a speed of 156 miles per hour it succeeded in beating specially designed racing machines. KLM were the first operators of the Douglas airliner in Europe.

the pilots. And there were the structural changes: an enlarged tail fin, a stronger, power-operated undercarriage.

Safety was also improved. Flying the traditional passenger planes could be an exhausting job and pilot fatigue contributed to many accidents. The typical trimotor had limited forward vision, thanks to the engine perched on the nose in front of the pilot. It threw oil, which spattered the windscreen, it deafened the pilot and vibrated the whole cockpit. Erratic engine performance, the crude and heavy flying controls and minimal instruments, kept the pilot on the edge of his seat. Even in good weather conditions, he could rarely afford to relax his grip on the control column. In bad weather, holding the aircraft straight and level could become an exhausting wrestling match.

On the DC-3, the pilot's controls were duplicated, so that the aircraft could be flown from either of the two cockpit seats. One of the most significant innovations was the first auto-pilot ever to be installed in an airliner. With this instrument switched on, the aircraft would maintain straight and level flight by using sensors to detect changes of attitude. Small corrections would be made by power-operation of the flying control surfaces. On long-haul flights, the crew could switch to auto pilot and rest, until a new course needed to be set, or until preparing for landing.

When the prototype was ready, the aircraft that emerged from the Santa Monica factory in December 1935, was effectively a new design.

A new innovation in the DC-3 was the duplication of the pilot's controls. Another was the automatic pilot, which can be seen in the centre of the instrument panel, above the engine throttle quadrant.

It was the third Douglas Commercial type – the DC-3, the sleeper version became the Douglas Sleeper Transport, or DST. The first flight of the DC-3 on 17 December 1935, came thirty two years to the day after the Wright Brothers first took to the air and marks the launch of the modern airliner, whose birth certificate had been the TWA letter to Donald Douglas, three years earlier. The DC-3 was not only bigger, it was also faster and far stronger than the DC-2. Its deep wing section gave a high degree of lift, and space for extra fuel tanks, which extended its range to over 3,600 miles. Its payload was more than two and a half tons. The cabin was spacious, soundproofed, and air-conditioned and the passengers loved it. America could now be crossed from coast to coast in less than 20 hours. American Airlines had got exactly what they asked for and it is a tribute to their detailed specification and to the Douglas engineers, that together they managed to envisage and build the perfect airliner. As with the DC-1, there were teething problems with the engines, but not the airframe. The 'prototype' was effectively the first production aircraft, nothing major needed to be changed.

Production began with the DST sleeper version, in which fourteen wealthy passengers could sleep the flight away. Its berths were in two tiers, the upper row could be folded up during daylight hours, while the lower row converted into seating. Privacy at night was provided by curtains and the upper level berths had their own small windows, also covered by curtains and designed to help reduce feelings of

The first of the many – Douglas Sleeper Transport NC 14988 DC-3 – which made its first flight in December 1935; seen here in the markings of American Airlines. The distictive outline had arrived!

claustrophobia. Although the flight could still be bumpy and any sleep was likely to be interrupted by refuelling stops, it was a glorious form of travel for the pampered few who could afford it. An intimate moment from a Douglas publicity film promoting the service, shows the stewardess smiling sweetly as she tucks one of her contented female passengers into bed. Next morning, she would be awoken by the stewardess bringing her breakfast in bed.

In August 1936, the first non-sleeper version of the DC-3 left the factory. It had twenty-one comfortable seats, laid out in rows of two-plus-one, with an off-set gangway. Each row of seats had its own large, rectangular window and, since flights were not made at high altitude, they offered superb views of America's great natural features. It was this version of the DC-3 that revolutionised the economics of passenger aircraft. At 11.3 tons, it weighed 50% more than any other airliner, but carried 33% more payload. At roughly 70 cents a mile, its operating costs were estimated to be about half the figure for a Ford Trimotor. Its improved range increased its earning ability since less time was wasted in refuelling stops, it could fly coast-to-coast with only two. Its non-stop New York – Chicago time of four hours made it possible for return business trips to be made between the two cities, without the need for an overnight stay. The train took 18 hours, one way.

At last the airlines had the aircraft they needed to make money and prices came down as passenger numbers began to go up. Mail

A Douglas Sleeper Transport operated by United Air Lines. Note the small oblong windows for the upper berths.

contracts were no longer essential to profitability and in 1936,
American Airlines turned its heavy losses into a modest profit. The
other airlines were soon clamouring for DC-3s, just as they had for
Boeing 247s only three years earlier. As President Franklin Roosevelt's
'New Deal' policies began to lift America out of the economic
depression that had blighted the country since the 'Wall Street Crash'
of 1929, the airline business began to boom. Competition on the most
popular routes, like New York – Chicago, became increasingly cut-
throat. In 1932 United Airlines had seemed to be holding all the aces,
with their monopoly on the Boeings. Now the tables had been turned
and they needed DC-3s if they were to survive. Unlike Boeing, whose
rebuff to TWA had launched the DC-1 project, Douglas was happy to
supply anybody who wanted his aircraft. By the start of 1937, United
were abandoning their Boeings and introducing the DC-3 on their key
routes. In February 1937, they launched the ultimate in luxury travel
on the Chicago route. The 'Sky Lounge' was a DC-3 with just fourteen
swivel armchairs. But it was not an economic proposition and was
soon withdrawn. The message was clear: the future of air travel lay
with high volume and low cost.

Public confidence in flying increased and most people no longer
dreaded the prospect of a mid-air structural failure. The DC-3 felt safe,
it could fly on one engine and insurance companies felt confident
enough to introduce automatic vending machines at the major
American airports. For a few dollars, you could insure your life before

Left: As competition between American airlines intensified, United Air Lines came up with a luxury travel incentive – the Sky Lounge service – fourteen swivel seats. **Right:** *A major part of airline business consisted of mail transport.*

flying – as long as your aircraft was a low-risk DC-3. This was the first popular and easily affordable air travel insurance – only now, with the DC-3 were insurers willing to take on the risk. This prompted the first recorded attempted murder on an airliner. A husband insured his wife's life for $5,000, before seeing her off on a DC-3. Later there was a mid-air explosion, as the bomb he had planted in her suitcase detonated. But he had underestimated the strength of her plane. Being a DC-3, it survived the blast and landed safely: the bomber was caught and the insurers kept their money.

Soon extraordinary stories of the aircraft's ability to survive disasters began to accumulate. One survived the loss of a wing tip in a mid-air collision, another hit an air pocket and dropped like a stone. Its passengers were hurled about and seats were even torn from their mountings. Yet an inspection of the airframe after landing revealed no signs of any damage, every single rivet had held. The strength of the DC-3 impressed the American Army. They already operated and trusted the military version of the DC-2 and Douglas were asked to produce a similar version of the DC-3 design.

In only a few years, passenger aircraft had changed out of all recognition. The draughty, noisy machines of the wood and fabric era now seemed like lumbering relics from another age and most were soon on a one-way flight to the scrapyard. The DC-3 was not just a good and safe aircraft to fly in, it also looked good. Many airlines made a feature of the smooth aluminium skin, polishing it to a mirror finish and decorating it with a variety of bold and eye-catching paint schemes. The DC-3 was an important move forward into the

AIR TRANSPORT IN WAR

The transport aircraft was a new phenomenon on the battlefield. In the later stages of World War One, large biplane bombers had been developed, but few seriously regarded aircraft as a practical proposition for the transport of stores and equipment or troops. By 1939, when the war in Europe began, Germany had discovered the value of transport aircraft. Their lumbering tri-motor, the Junkers Ju 52, had been developed – like the C-47 – as a peacetime airliner. It was already obsolete when the war began, but was still able to demonstrate its versatility as a troop transport, a freighter and a launching platform for parachute assaults.

Being slow and usually unarmed, the transport aircraft was always vulnerable to attack and losses could be devastatingly high. A flight of Ju 52s en route to North Africa were caught over the Mediterranean by Allied fighters and all shot down. In one horrific example of mistaken identity, twenty-four C-47s, fully loaded with American paratroops, were shot down by American forces over Italy. But, despite their vulnerability, transports played an increasingly vital role in every theatre of the war.

The C-47 was adopted as the standard Allied transport aircraft and became the basic tool for a whole range of tasks. Without the C-47, it's hard to imagine how the Second World War could have been fought. While bombers and fighters were modified or superseded, as technology and tactics changed, the simple and rugged C-47 remained in production and in the thick of the action throughout.

streamline era. Industrial designers began to copy its rounded shape, sharp angles vanished. Everything – from toasters and refrigerators, to cars and railway locomotives, became curved and aerodynamic. As America fought its way out of the despair of the Great Depression, flying caught the mood of the time. The shining and shapely DC-3 was an uplifting symbol of President Roosevelt's New Deal. He told the American people they had 'nothing to fear but fear itself' and the DC-3 seemed to express that mood of returning confidence and of the modern age. By 1939, 90% of the world's airline passengers were flying in DC-3s. Like Henry Ford's 'Model T' car, which gave ordinary people the freedom of the open road, the DC-3 opened up the skies to them.

Few machines manage to re-invent the wheel, yet the DC-3 did it – not once but twice. In the 1930s it revolutionised civil air transport: in the 1940s it revolutionised the whole art of warfare. In December 1941, Japan launched its surprise attack on Pearl Harbour and America was catapulted into a war it had tried hard to keep out of. Sixteen days later, the US Army Air Force took delivery of its very first C-47. It was the military version of the DC-3, which had been ordered back in 1940. As with the C-33/DC-2 conversion, it featured a strengthened cargo floor and a pair of wide loading doors at the rear. The interior was stark and functional, without soundproofing, heating or any of the refinements of the DC-3. It was not even lined, revealing all the details of its construction. It was simply a 'flying truck', an empty tube to be

Mass production American style.

packed with whatever the military decided it needed to shift. It was expected that the Government would adopt the DC-3 as a military transport. What wasn't expected was the sheer scale of the operation. By the end of the war, some 10,000 C-47s had rolled off the Douglas production lines. The Russians also built more than 2,000 examples and even Japan built nearly 500, having signed a pre war licence with Douglas.

As the American Government came to terms with the shock of Pearl Harbour, the economy was placed on a war footing. It was clear that air power would play a central role in American strategy. It was a devastating surprise attack from the air that had left Pearl Harbour a smoking ruin, and America's failure to intercept it, taught her top military planners some very painful lessons. President Roosevelt appealed to Congress for a massive allocation of funds, to equip America with a gigantic airborne armada of bombers, fighters and transports. Aircraft builders like Boeing and Douglas turned over their entire production capacity to the war effort. Other industries switched from the production of peace-time goods to manufacturing aircraft components and sub-assemblies. The sheer scale of the operation was awe-inspiring and daunting, but the mass-production methods perfected by Henry Ford's car plants in Detroit had already been widely adopted by American industry before the war and Douglas had already turned out more than 500 DC-3s.

With spare capacity at the Santa Monica plant already fully

Women played an increasingly important role in American aircraft plants, although the spotless outfit of this C-47 engine fitter suggests that she may be a carefully posed model.

committed to bomber production, Douglas set up a new factory in Long Beach California, dedicated to the C-47. As the orders poured in from the military, it soon became obvious that even more capacity would be needed and another huge factory was set up at Tulsa, Oklahoma. But until the new plants could begin full-scale production, other solutions had to be found.

Since earliest times, civilians have found themselves dragooned into military service, while their horses and farm carts provided improvised transport. As war became mechanised, the process continued. During the First World War, fighting men were conscripted, while London buses and Parisian taxis were commandeered to transport them to the Front. As America prepared once more to fight a war in Europe, civil airliners were the obvious stop-gap source of air transport. All new DC-3s on the Santa Monica assembly line were impressed into military service, while the existing airline fleets were decimated, with 10% of all DC-3s requisitioned by the military. The luxury seating, the kitchen equipment, even the toilet, were unceremoniously ripped out. The polished metal exteriors, with their smart liveries and proud slogans, were covered with a coat of standard G. I. (Government Issue) olive drab paint. The DC-3 Flagships of American Airlines became anonymous C-47s, serving alongside other former airliners from United, Pan American, TWA and many others.

The final indignity came when their new passengers – the American soldiers, who adopted the G.I. name tag – hit on their own name for the C-47. American warplanes all had their official number, but most

NOSE ART

The crews of most wartime aircraft liked to embellish them with a name and a suitably eye-catching piece of artwork. The process was evidence of the strong sense of bonding that develops between a good 'ship' and its crew. In the days of sailing ships, going to sea was always a gamble, the crew would put their trust in God and in the carved figurehead mounted on the ship's bow. It was usually female and well-endowed. She acted as a kind of guardian angel, watching over the ship and protecting the crew.

The aircrews in World War Two needed all the protection they could get and instinctively created their own figureheads, in the form of a name and a mascot painted on the nose of the aircraft. Most were shapely females in varying states of undress. The sentiments of the crews were much the same regardless of the aircraft. The unarmed and docile C-47 could still carry 'nose art' as racy and profane as any fighter. The girls were long-legged and big-busted, with inviting names like 'Easy Pick Up' or 'Classy Chassis'. Some aircrews adopted cartoon characters which were usually a wry expression of the daily grind, with references to aching backs and shattered nerves. 'War Weary' was a C-47 adorned with an exhausted Donald Duck. One simply carried the single word 'Why?' But a stork delivering a baby and the slogan 'Anything Anytime Anywhere' seemed to sum up the C-47's role best.

One C-47 was named 'Old Miscellaneous'. When retired from front-line duty in 1944, it was sent on a triumphal fund-raising tour of the United States. It was only the tenth C-47 delivered to the Army and had flown some 2,000 missions. It had been through twelve sets of engines and had been given new wing tips, elevators and rudder. Its fuselage was pock-marked with battle damage from small arms and shrapnel splinters. In the cabin, a small plate was fixed which read, *'This ship is the oldest C-47 in the Pacific and one of the most courageous. Treat her kindly and she will always get you to your destination'*. To the Army the C-47 was just a number, but to the crews she had a heart and a soul.

also had a suitably aggressive name. So the B17 was the 'Flying Fortress', the P47 fighter was the 'Thunderbolt'. There were Avengers, Invaders, Warhawks and Havocs, but the C-47 became the 'Gooney Bird' – named after a large and ungainly inhabitant of the Pacific, which got airborne with much difficulty and a lot of flapping!

Airliners which once carried Hollywood film stars, politicians and self-made millionaires across America, were now just another 'Gooney' to be used and abused by the military. But beneath the olive drab uniformity, emotions were beginning to stir and soon a strange love/hate relationship would grow up between the G.I. and his aircraft. For the C-47 was very much the property of the regular soldier. Gung-ho fighter pilots and bomber crews might have their own favourites and would argue fiercely, with their fists if necessary, the merits of the Fortress against the Liberator, the Mustang versus the Thunderbolt. But the universal soldier 'G.I. Joe', soon learned which aircraft he could depend on, it was the 'Gooney' every time. It would fly him into battle, bring in his ammunition, his equipment, his fuel and his rations. If he was wounded, it would fly him back to safety. Sure it was slow, it rattled and shook and it lacked even the basic comforts. But it was his aircraft.

As the C-47 construction programme began to roll, a new American folk heroine, was starting to make her mark, alongside 'G.I. Joe'. 'Rosie the Riveter' was a generic term, coined for all the women who suddenly found themselves drafted into the aircraft factories to help their 'Uncle Sam' to win the air war. At the Douglas Long Beach plant,

some two thirds of the workers were women. Urged on by banners bearing patriotic slogans and American flags draped above their work benches, the army of construction workers toiled away. They worked long hours and the pace was relentless.

Each C-47 required the drilling of thousands upon thousands of holes, row after row of them, in hundreds of sheets of aluminium and the fixing together of those sheets by a rivet in every single hole, about 500,000 rivets in total. Deafened by the endless chatter of the pneumatic rivet guns, the 'Rosies' toiled away. Most had no previous experience of factory work. They came from colleges, from offices, from hearth and home. Often they had husbands or sweethearts fighting in Europe or the Pacific and the chance to do something constructive to help them was a very important morale booster.

Pre-war ideas about 'women's work' had to be revised, when it became obvious that the women could drill and rivet every bit as well as the men. Aircraft building involves precision and consistency if individual components and sub assemblies are to be interchangeable. Since aluminium is a light metal which, unlike steel, needs a fairly light touch, the more heavy-handed male industrial workers often proved to be unsuitable for aircraft work. Many women, thrown into the male-dominated world of the shop floor, discovered they were actually better than a lot of the men at working to fine limits.

When the new factories were completed and the workforce had been trained, C-47 deliveries soon got up to speed. Production

'Rosie the Riveter' in action on a C-47 cockpit section.

eventually reached the astonishing rate of one new aircraft every thirty four minutes. The C-47 transport was far less complicated to build than the fighters and bombers, with their sophisticated weapons systems and highly stressed airframes, yet it could stand up to the harsh conditions of the battlefield much better than many of the more complex machines. The Douglas design philosophy could be summed up as 'little and often'. Hundreds of small bolts and thousands of rivets spread the load and avoided the use of expensive, high-tensile components. By over-engineering the airframe, Douglas had produced a machine which rarely suffered a structural failure and could be easily maintained with basic hand tools. An entire wing could be removed with nothing more than a couple of spanners and enough patience to undo the 328 securing bolts.

When the 2,000th C-47 left the Long Beach factory on 2nd October 1942, it was signed by all the women who had worked on its construction. The Douglas company suggested to the Army that, as a morale-boosting exercise, a coat of clear varnish could be applied over the signatures and the aircraft put into service unpainted. The Military flatly refused to even consider such a far-fetched idea and regulation olive drab soon obliterated the names. The aircraft was then despatched to the Pacific and forgotten. But soon a steady trickle of letters from American G.I.s began to find their way to the Douglas factory. They were addressed to 'Lou', or 'Wilma', or 'Patsy' and they wanted details: who were they, what was their phone number, could

As the C-47s roll off the production line, the Douglas work force are reminded that America will 'win with wings'.

they send their vital statistics? Protected by the paint, the signatures had survived and could still just be made out by the mechanics and air crews who worked on the aircraft during its travels in the Pacific. The 'Rosies' often left inviting messages hidden inside the aircraft they helped to build. Many a wartime romance began with a lucky mechanic discovering one inside a wing, or on the back of an inspection cover.

As the huge fleet of C-47s passed into the hands of the military, it took a while for their extraordinary versatility to sink in. The military mind tends to like order and insists on classification of all equipment. An organisation which stamps a folding table as 'Table – Wood – Folding – Bedside' was likely to stick some equally exact label on the C-47. Its two main functions were to be as a transporter of urgent supplies and as a troop carrier. It would also be used for casualty evacuation. Its cabin could be fitted out with 28 folding canvas seats, or filled with cargo, secured to tie-down rings on the floor. It could be turned into a flying ambulance by fitting 14 stretcher berths – an austere echo of its original role as a luxury sleeper transport for American Airlines. Sadly for the G.I.s, there would be no hostess service or breakfast in bed.

It was decided soon after America's entry into the war, that the standard Allied transport aircraft should be the C-47. Britain's Royal Air Force began taking delivery of the type and christened it the 'Dakota', a name which is still widely used today. Like the American

BURMA

The most striking example of the C-47's ability to supply an entire military operation came in Burma. Having lost the territory to the Japanese during their whirlwind advance through South East Asia, the British were determined to recover it. Much of the country is dense jungle, without any road access. Any attempt to supply an army fighting its way through this terrain would be fraught with problems. One method of overcoming the lack of ground transport was devised by the British Major General Orde Wingate. He established a force of jungle fighters, known as 'Chindits'. His unorthodox approach involved establishing isolated 'Citadels' behind the Japanese lines, supplied entirely by air.

A fleet of C-47s was used to drop stores and equipment by parachute into clearings in the jungle. On the ground, teams of mules would be used to ferry the supplies through the dense undergrowth to the battlefront. It was dangerous work for the C-47 crews, with no hope of landing if anything went wrong. The dispatchers, pushing the heavy para-packs out of the open rear doors, had a particularly risky job, but casualties were surprisingly light. The operation was unlike any previous campaign and the results were impressive but, at the height of his success, Wingate was killed when his aircraft ploughed into a mountain. Ironically, it was one of his lifelines – a C-47.

G.I., the British 'Tommy' soon developed a respect and affection for the transport. In the harsh world of the distant battlefield, the welcome sight of a 'Dak' coming in could mean a brief respite from duty and a link with home. It brought the mail, or food parcels, or just the items of equipment which made life that little bit easier. For some it meant survival, many a wounded man owed his life to that bumpy flight back to the base hospital and safety.

When the United States Army Air Force – the USAAF – formed the Air Transport Command in 1942, the almost infinite possibilities of air transport began to be fully realised. Soon the entire operation was built around the versatility of the C-47. Air supply on the battlefield had originally been seen as rather like an extension of the air mail service – a quick way to deliver small quantities of lightweight, urgently needed items of equipment, like medical supplies. But as the war progressed and the numbers of C-47s grew, they began to be taken for granted. As they proved their ability, they were given tougher assignments and were soon expected to carry whatever could be fitted inside without grossly exceeding the 6,000lb load limit. This could mean anything – from a jeep and trailer, or an anti tank gun, to a mountain of ammunition boxes or scores of fuel cans.

There seemed to be no limit to what the C-47 could cope with. Its low landing speed of 60 mph and its short take-off run of 1,000 ft, meant that it could operate from almost any airfield and the C-47

RAF Dakotas come to the rescue of a Wingate column. Wounded and sick Chindits being airlifted to hospital in India after being picked up at a makeshift landing strip in the Burmese jungle.

became a vital lifeline for troops fighting in remote locations. Soon the former airliner, which had been designed for use on tarmac runways, was being treated more like an off-road truck. Fully loaded C-47s were bumped down on rough airstrips, hacked from the jungles of Burma. Lurching over the baked dessert sand of the Sahara in a cloud of dust, they delivered in hours, what would have taken days by road, except that there were no roads anyway.

One of their most demanding and dangerous operations was 'flying the Hump', the supply run from Burma to China. It involved taking the unpressurised C-47s up to high altitude, to avoid the mountain peaks of the Himalayas. They would regularly have to fly through ice storms, snow storms, heavy rain, tornadoes and typhoons. To add to the fun there were always marauding Japanese fighters, ready to shoot down any of the unarmed C-47s they could find. Very occasionally it was the other way round. During one attack, a Japanese 'Zero' fighter accidentally rammed a C-47. A huge section of the transport's roof was torn off, but it flew on. The Zero cartwheeled into a mountain and exploded. One Japanese fighter pilot decided to capture the C-47 he had intercepted. Flying alongside, he indicated that it should follow him back to his base. But he had the misfortune to position himself on the wrong side of the C-47, opposite its loading door. Without warning, it flew open and he was blasted out of the sky by a machine gun the C-47 crew had set up in the doorway.

British and Indian troops on hand to load supplies aboard C-47s. British and American insignia are evident on these two aircraft.

In 1942, the USAAF's Troop Carrier Command officially adopted the C-47 as the standard paratrooping aircraft and it was in its parachute-dropping role that the C-47 was to make its most crucial contribution to the war. A parachute operation requires two basic ingredients: brave and highly trained men in the peak of physical condition and an aircraft they can jump from with confidence. The men are not a problem, any elite unit will attract strong competition among soldiers wanting to become part of it. It is then a matter of weeding out all but the very best of them. The aircraft is not so easy to get right.

The first drops were made from biplanes, the parachutists actually walking out along the lower wing, before letting go. Later, they dropped through a hatch in the floor, but neither method was satisfactory. Speed is vital during a drop: if the troops are to avoid being widely scattered, they must leave the aircraft in quick succession. The C-47, with its side door, was to provide the ideal jump platform. With their parachutes opened automatically by a static line anchored to the aircraft, the paratroops soon perfected a technique of exiting at speed. Eighteen men would pass through the door in less than ten seconds. Once on the ground, the paratroops have to be entirely self-sufficient in equipment. This meant that, in addition to his main and reserve parachutes, each man was loaded down with a mass of equipment, weighing as much as 130 lb. But there were some items

The Dakota/C-47 Skytrain became the workhorse of RAF Transport Command and the USAAF. It could be found in every theatre of the war.

that were too heavy or bulky for a man to jump with. These would be dropped in separate 'parapacks'. At first these were pushed out of the door after the troops, but soon a system was devised by which up to six packs could be slung under the aircraft. These were then released by the crew as the men jumped, in the hope that all would land together – they rarely did!

The first major Airborne Operation was during the invasion of Sicily in July 1943, when almost 4,000 paratroops were dropped by a fleet of C-47 transports. Then came Italy and, in June 1944, the invasion of mainland Europe – 'D-Day'. The invasion was to be the largest airborne operation ever attempted. Some 17,000 American and 7,000 British paratroops were to be dropped. A fleet of nearly 900 C-47s was assembled to transport these, the first troops to liberate Europe.

C-47 Skytrains from the 438th Troop Carrier Group, lined up at RAF Greenham Common during the assault on mainland Europe in the summer of 1944.

Chapter Four

DROP ZONE

'When you land in Normandy, you'll have only one friend: God.' These were the daunting words of Brigadier General James 'Jumpin Jim' Gavin in his training sessions to the hundreds of men of the 505th Regiment of the 82nd Airborne. They had volunteered for one of the riskiest stages of one of the most daring operations of the Second World War – as paratroop pathfinders. These men would be the first to jump into occupied Europe, behind Hitler's 'impregnable' Atlantic Wall. They would set up the radios and marker beacons to guide the remaining planes bringing in the paratroop force that would unleash the D-Day invasion. If the pathfinder operation went wrong, or if they put their lights in the wrong place, then this could spell disaster for the rest of the night-time para drop. This could in turn transform D-Day into a tragedy. The pathfinders would have to display supreme courage and resolution. And the unarmed C-47s that carried the pathfinders would have to be flown with pinpoint accuracy.

Planning for D-Day had been going on for years. In January 1944, General Dwight D. Eisenhower was appointed Supreme Commander, Allied Expeditionary Force. On his shoulders fell the final military

A well known press picture of men of the 22nd Independent Parachute Company synchronising their watches on the night of 5 June 1944.

responsibility for the Allied invasion of Europe. In five frantic months Ike, as he was affectionately known, transformed the D-Day plans into a mighty operation in which 175,000 men from 9 Allied divisions would land on and behind five beaches along the Normandy coast. More than 5,000 ships would be needed to transport these men and the supplies they would require across the English Channel – including 55,000 vehicles ranging from motorcycles to tanks. 11,000 planes would support the invasion by protecting the ships, bombing the enemy command and control centres and ensuring mastery of the skies so that on the day itself the Luftwaffe were not able to offer any threat to the invasion at its most vulnerable time, as the men struggled ashore to establish a beachhead. The invasion would be a combined American, British and Canadian operation. The Free French, Poles and Norwegians would also take part. Minute by minute planning and synchronisation would be necessary. It would be the largest amphibious landing in history across sixty to a hundred miles of one of the roughest and most unpredictable seas in the world. And amphibious landings were highly dangerous military operations.

There had been various successful invasions prior to D-Day – in North Africa, Sicily and in Italy. But none of these had been against fortified coastlines. Facing the Allies on D-Day was the huge defensive structure called the Atlantic Wall. Millions of tons of concrete and steel had gone into constructing beach defences. Miles of barbed wire had

With every day that passed, the defences along the Normandy coast were improved by the Germans, under the thorough and enthusiastic direction of Field Marshal Rommel.

been laid. From giant pill boxes, machine guns and 88 mm howitzers were positioned to unleash a murderous fire across any beach that might be a landing zone. Four million mines had been laid. And waiting well behind the beaches were some of the toughest panzer divisions in the German army. Churchill called the invasion 'the most difficult and complicated operation ever to take place.' If it succeeded, the Allies would have opened the long awaited Second Front in Europe, second to the gargantuan struggle that was taking place on the Eastern Front. If it failed, and the Germans were able to throw the Allies back into the sea, this would be an unparalleled disaster to the Allied cause and would almost certainly prolong the war for some years – or even force the Allies into a negotiated settlement with Hitler. The invasion of Europe was a gigantic risk. Eisenhower knew perfectly well what was a stake and how the future of the war depended upon his success.

In planning for the beach landings it became clear that some sort of flank protection was going to be necessary. In the west, this meant protecting the men of the US 4th Division as they waded ashore onto Utah beach, from a German counter attack across the marshes at the head of the Cotentin peninsula. In the east, this involved protecting the flank of Sword beach, both from a German counter attack across the Orne river and also from the German heavy guns situated at Merville that could rain death and destruction down onto the invading British

The Allied invasion was expected in the Pas de Calais area but German defences all along the Channel coast were strengthened right up to the month of June 1944.

forces. This was a perfect task for paratroopers and their objectives were to seize and control certain key targets and to hold onto these targets against whatever the Germans might throw at them until relieved. The paratroopers would be dropped through the night that preceeded the dawn invasion.

As the plans were worked through in detail, the full risks of the airborne operation became clear. The Germans had formidable defences and were at the very least alert to an invasion possibility. There were machine guns positioned to provide fire across many possible landing sites. Anti-glider and paratrooper defences, known as 'Asparagus' from their appearance, littered the Normandy countryside. Many areas outside immediate road and communication corridors were mined. In the west, the Germans had opened the locks along the Merderet river and much of the drop zone for the Americans was flooded. As if these dangers were not enough, the paratroop drop would take place at night in darkness when pilots and paratroopers would have maximum difficulty in locating where they were and where they should be. And as each man had to be self-sufficient on the ground, every paratrooper carried some 130 lbs of kit and equipment. Only the finest men could be expected to perform well in these circumstances.

Soon after America entered the war the US Army had formed two paratroop divisions. The 82nd Airborne Division was known as the

American parachute troops make their first public appearance at Fort Benning, USA. Recruiting for a parachute battalion had begun. The C-47 was proving to be the ideal aircraft for airborne drops.

'All American' and the 101st Airborne was known as the 'Screaming Eagles'. With them, the IX Troop Carrier Command was formed to train C-47 pilots to drop the paras. All paratroopers were volunteers. They wanted to be the best and went through a gruelling training regime. As many as two out of three volunteers dropped out during this training that included 136 mile hikes carrying full equipment and three-day forced marches. Paratroopers had to be supremely fit and mentally very alert. After five practice jumps, a soldier qualified and received his paratrooper wings.

The 82nd Airborne had been in combat in Sicily and Italy but the 101st, like most of the other units in training for D-Day, had yet to experience their baptism of fire. The training continued relentlessly through the winter of 1943 and the spring of 1944. Training, training and more training. As their targets were identified, models of the Cotentin peninsula were made. When each unit was allocated its precise instructions, the men went through their orders over and over again. There is a special espirit de corps in paratroop units. Partly because of the extraordinary bravery needed by every man. Partly because all paratroopers, from generals to privates, share the same risks and danger of the parachute jump. The men of the 82nd and 101st would need all the espirit they could muster to take on what they all realised was their greatest challenge. Finally, after a delay of 24 hours due to bad weather, Eisenhower made the fateful decision to go. D-

The 'Screaming Eagles' put on an impressive display for the British Prime Minister, Winston Churchill, who visited them at Newbury in Berkshire some three months prior to D-Day.

Day was set for 6th June and the paras would go in the night before. There would be a bright, nearly full moon that night and everyone hoped for clear weather.

As the afternoon of 5th June turned to dusk, at airfields across southern England paratroopers packed and repacked their equipment and company commanders went through detailed orders for the umpteenth time. At Greenham Common, a long line of C-47s waited on the tarmac to carry their human cargo behind the enemy lines. As the men of the 101st Airborne prepared to emplane, a surprise visitor turned up. General Eisenhower chose to spend the last minutes before the invasion with the paratroopers. His advisors had predicted casualty rates as high as eighty percent. But he wanted to look the men in the eye who would lead his invasion force. 'I've done all I can do, now it's up to you,' Ike told one captain. Eisenhower mingled with the men and tried to encourage them. Some of them had painted their faces using Red Indian-type warpaint. Others had their hair shaved into mohican-style cuts. One later said he thought it was Ike's morale that was improved by being with these gung-ho young paras. When Ike questioned a para from his home state of Kansas the soldier was so terrified at being addressed by the Supreme Commander that he dried up and couldn't even remember his own name! As he left them to board the C-47s, one soldier called out 'Now quit worrying, General, we'll take care of this thing for you.' When he returned to his staff car,

General Eisenhower with the paratroopers.

his driver later remembered that tears welled up in his eyes. 'Well,' he mused quietly, 'it's on.'

As the twilight turned into darkness, the paratroopers clambered aboard their C-47s. Most of them were carrying so much equipment that they had to be hauled or pushed up into the plane. The best pilots, men like Adam Parsons of the IX Troop Carrier Command, had been selected to drop the pathfinders. 'I went back and shook hands with every one of them on board,' remembered Parsons. But as he took off he felt uneasy that 'something might happen that would foul everything up.' The pathfinder planes took off at about 10.00 pm and went in about an hour or so before the main body of aircraft. Flying exceptionally low after crossing the French coast they still attracted heavy anti-aircraft fire. They navigated visually from point to point and having identified the drop zone with total accuracy they dropped the 'eyes' of the invasion from about 300 feet. The parachutes of the pathfinders barely had time to open before the men hit the ground. As he landed, Private Bob Murphy of the 505th felt a sense of intense exhilaration and thought to himself 'Now the war's on.'

Bob Murphy rolled over on landing and found himself in a small garden. The owner, a sixty year old French school mistress came out to see what all the noise was about. Facing this 19 year old paratrooper all blacked up and laden down with kit, the school teacher was frozen to the spot with terror. Murphy put a finger over his lips to make a

LIST OF WHAT EVERY AMERICAN PARATROOPER CARRIED

Every American paratrooper had to be self-sufficient when he landed and carried a heavy array of equipment with him into battle which included:

One jump suit, boots, gloves, Mae West, main parachute, reserve parachute, rifle, .45 automatic pistol, trench knife, jump knife, hunting knife, machete, one cartridge belt, two bandoliers, two cans of machine gun ammunition, one Hawkins mine – capable of blowing off the track of a tank, four blocks of TNT, one entrenching tool, three first aid kits, two morphine needles, one gas mask, a canteen of water, three day's supply of K rations, two day's supply of D rations, six fragmentation grenades, one Gammon grenade, one orange and one red smoke grenade, one blanket, one raincoat, one change of socks and underwear, two cartons of cigarettes, one helmet.

gesture of 'silence' and slipped away quietly. Murphy and the pathfinders of the 505th had had a perfect drop just on the edge of St Mère Église. The pilots had taken them to the exact point. Now they set about marking the drop zones with automatic direction finder radios, and beacon lights laid out in T formations along the ground. They moved swiftly and efficiently to fulfill the tasks they had trained for. They didn't have long to wait before the sky was filled with the sound of the main fleet of hundreds of C-47s overhead. The drop was planned to start about 1.15 am.

Each C-47 carried its complement of 18 paratroopers. Some of them were quiet – anxiously thinking about what was going to happen to them. More than one thought 'If I'm going to die, please God, let me die like a man.' Others expressed their pent-up tension in singing. In one C-47, Jack Norton had a 10-note harmonica which he got out and played vigorously. The men joined in a passionate and loud sing-song. 'There was a lot of nervous energy, a lot of it,' remembers Norton. Elsewhere, the paras were mostly quiet. Some prayed silently. A few played cards. A few managed to read. One or two amazed their fellows by falling asleep, despite the tension – perhaps more a result of the side effects of the airsickness pills that had been handed out before take-off than of supremely cool heads. 'If anyone tells you they weren't scared he's a liar, a big liar,' remembers Bill Katzenstein.

The pilots of the C-47s were afraid, also. Many of them had not

Men of the US 101st Airborne on the eve of D-Day. Note the crudely painted invasion stripes in front of the C-47's tailplane.

flown in combat before. Nor had they been trained for night flying or how to cope with anti-aircraft fire. They were also terrified of colliding with neighbouring aircraft. More than 800 C-47s were flying in a huge armada some 300 miles long, nine planes wide. Each group flew in a V formation with only 100 feet between wingtips. Only 1,000 feet separated one V formation of nine C-47s from the next V behind. There was complete radio silence and only the lead plane in every five V formations displayed a show of lights at its rear to guide the others. For aircraft that were 65 feet long and 95 feet wide from wingtip to wingtip, this was remarkably tight formation flying. It called upon the maximum skill and concentration from the tense, nervous pilots. And, totally unarmed, they were on course to cross into heavily defended enemy territory.

Nevertheless, this huge armada of C-47s assembled over southern England exactly as planned and headed out across the Channel, flying at 500 feet to escape German radar detection. Sixty miles out in the Channel, a British submarine lay on the surface sending out a beacon light. This was the signal for the C-47s to turn sharply left to the south east. This they all did in near perfect formation and passed between the Channel Islands of Jersey and Guernsey. A few minutes later they crossed the western coast of the Cotentin peninsula. Now they were over enemy territory and, still in formation without radio contact, they dropped to 600 feet which was the designated height for the drop.

The evening of D-Day and this C-47 takes off from Greenham Common with a glider in tow. they are transporting part of an anti-aircraft battalion for the 82nd US Airborne.

Now, however, their real troubles began. Although the night had
been a clear one up to now, the remains of the storm that had delayed
D-Day by 24 hours were still passing through. As they crossed the
French coast they hit a thick bank of cloud, which the pilots flying in
the pathfinders had also encountered but because of the requirement
for radio silence they had not been able to pass back a warning to the
oncoming armada. As they lost sight of the planes only a few yards
from either wingtip, many pilots instinctively broke out of the close
formation they had flown in since England. Some of them descended,
others gained height; some peeled off to the right, others to the left.
After a few minutes they emerged from the bank of clouds. To the
amazement of some of the pilots they found themselves alone in the
sky. They had veered away from the vast formations they had been
part of which had just disappeared from view. Fighter pilots knew this
experience well – how the sky could be full of feuding aircraft one
minute and seemingly empty the next. But most of the C-47 pilots had
never known anything like it before. 'We were all alone,' remembered
one amazed paratrooper standing by the rear door. 'Where had all
those C-47s gone?'

Most pilots had no time to think about what to do. The moment
they emerged from the clouds the anti-aircraft batteries opened up on
them from the ground. The sky was filled with tracers and explosions
from anti-aircraft fire. The tracers outlined red, yellow and blue arcs in

On their way – men of the 101st US Airborne – mixed emotions are registered on their faces.

the sky. Searchlights came up from across the French countryside. Most of the pilots and paratroopers who witnessed this described it as the greatest Fourth of July firework show they had ever seen. But many pilots, now severely disoriented by the cloud and the unexpected heaviness of the flak, speeded up. They were supposed to approach the drop zones at 90 miles per hour, at 600 feet, in order to drop the paras accurately on the right spot. Now, many throttled up to 150 miles per hour. Some dropped to a few hundred feet, others rose to nearly 2,000 feet trying to get above the flak.

Meanwhile, inside the diving and weaving C-47s, the paras began their final checks and jump procedure. Each plane carried a jumpmaster who stood by the open rear door. 'Stand up and hook up' was his first shouted order above the roar of the engines and the sound of the flak, some of which seemed horribly near to the men. Each para stood and attached his main parachute by a hook to a taught cable that was slung down the middle of the fuselage. This would automatically pull open his chute as he jumped from the plane. 'Sound off for equipment check,' shouted the jumpmaster and from up the plane would come the call sign from each man 'Eighteen OK,' 'Seventeen OK,' and so on down the line. They had practised this routine dozens of times before but never under fire and never knowing that they were about to jump into history.

With everything and everyone ready there was a final tense wait as

A 'stick' of parachute infantry awaiting the signal to jump from their C-47 Skytrain. They are hooked up to the static line down the centre of the fuselage; which will pull open their 'chutes as they drop away from the aircraft.

the planes twisted and turned trying to find the drop zones. Men fell over in the chaos. Others waited, terrified, as bullets and tracer tore past the aircraft. Some received direct hits in the wings or the fuselage but the C-47 could take the punishment and the pilots flew on with their mission. 'Of all the training we had,' one para remembered, 'nothing had prepared us for this.'

The pilots cued the paras with two lights. The red light was a signal to stand-by and most pilots put this on soon after they crossed the French coast. The green light was the signal to jump. But by now many of the pilots were hopelessly lost and confused. It should have taken them ten to fifteen minutes from crossing the coast to arriving at the drop zones. But flying out of formation through intense flak for fifteen minutes required a very cool head. Many pilots, frankly, didn't hang around to wait. They flashed the green light as soon as they thought they could. At the back of aircraft the jumpmaster screamed 'Go!' and the stick of paratroopers jumped out of the rear door in ten seconds as they had been trained. The speed with which such heavily loaded men were able to jump amazed those who witnessed it. With each man pushing into the back of the man in front, the routine was called the 'Airborne Shuffle'. Now for thousands of paratroopers thrown out into the night sky, as Bob Murphy had felt an hour before, the war was really on.

Those who had the misfortune to be dropped from C-47s which had speeded up and were flying faster than the intended 90 miles per hour were in the greatest immediate difficulty. Jack Norton jumped from a plane flying at such speed that as soon as he left the aircraft everything attached to his harness broke loose, pulled off by the static shock as his chute opened. He lost his father's precious First World War revolver. Packs of ammunition flew through his webbing and tore his kit, disappearing into the darkness below. He landed with such force that he was knocked unconscious. Coming around a few seconds later, Norton did a quick check and found that at least no bones were broken but his weapon and all of his ammunition were missing. 'I wasn't too well equipped to fight a war,' he modestly recalled later.

Most of the paratroopers were on the ground in a second or two, stunned by the experience of jumping into a barrage of tracer and anti-aircraft fire. Each man who landed safely now went into the next well practised drill of rolling up his parachute, hiding it and then assembling his rifle from the sections it had been dismantled into for the jump. Then they would go through the routine of 'rolling up the stick'. The reason for the speed of the 'Airborne Shuffle' was to ensure that men would land near to one another and could regroup quickly on the ground. Those who had jumped first would follow the line of the C-47 and those who jumped last would head in the other direction. In training, the stick of eighteen men then all met around the central trooper. But many paras who had jumped from speeding aircraft were now hopelessly separated and strung out across the French countryside. Many of them, too, were far from their drop zones. They had all learned the names of the villages and the farms in their zone and had memorised orders for where to assemble. But for many, the names they now saw meant nothing to them. Some of those who had maps found that they were off the edge of them. Having been dropped miles from the drop zone, they did not even know in which direction to head to find their nighttime objectives. One company was spread across twelve miles of countryside. A few, exhausted and drained by the experience, found a haystack or a barn to settle down in and did the only thing they could do – wait for daybreak, when they hoped to make some sense out of the situation.

Others had fared even worse. Many paras of the 82nd had jumped to the west of St Mère Église, astride the Merderet river where the Germans had flooded the valley. But Allied reconnaissance photographs had failed to distinguish between grass and the flooded fields. Landing fully laden in even three feet of water was too much for an unlucky few. Unable to detach themselves from their harnesses and

C-47s unload their human cargo over Hitler's Festung Europa. *They proved to be a steady platform from which to drop men and supplies.*

drawn along by the wind, they were dragged under and drowned in only a few feet of water. In all, 36 men drowned in the shallow waters of the Merderet during the night. About a dozen more were dropped over the Channel itself and drowned within seconds. 173 paratroopers broke a leg or an arm during landing.

Almost everyone who jumped that night had a story to tell. Fred Morgan Jnr, a medic with the 505th, had jumped in Sicily and Italy and both times the landings had been perfect. This time he landed in a tree. Struggling to free himself as the weight of his kit started slowly to pull him downwards, he felt the risers of his harness begin to strangle him. He reached for the knife that was inside a pocket near his collar to cut himself free but he was so nervous he dropped it. He knew he only had a few seconds left when he heard someone approach the tree. Trained never to call out, he decided this time to risk everything – as he was sure to be strangled by the harness soon, anyway. To his relief it was another American who quickly climbed into the tree and cut him free from the harness straps.

On the edge of the flooded Merderet river, one young trooper struggled vainly to find another American with whom he could join up. After a while he walked almost straight into the tommy gun of a man he had had a fight with in a pub in England and who had vowed to settle the score with him in Normandy. Of all people to bump into along the drop zone, he could not believe his bad luck. But both young men instantly decided that having survived so far, bygones would be bygones. They hugged and slapped each on the back and set off to defeat Hitler.

One paratrooper, hopelessly lost, eventually met up with another trooper. But he was amazed to find that this man was not from his company, was not from his battalion, was not even from his division. Men from the 82nd and 101st were jumbled up across the Cotentin peninsula but now had to reorganise and try to attain their objectives. In the worst recorded case, the commander of one battalion landed so far from everyone else that he did not see another American for five days!

For those on the ground a long night lay ahead. Paratroopers began to recover from the trauma of the jump and to organise. Everywhere officers went in search of their men and where units had become jumbled, ad hoc command structures were put in place. General Maxwell Taylor, commander of the 101st Division, spent twenty minutes trying to find another paratrooper. Eventually he met up with a private whom he hugged. Then, trying to locate their assembly point

ST MÈRE ÉGLISE

St Mère Église, where the first pathfinders had landed with pinpoint accuracy, was one of the major objectives of the first night. Situated on the main road from Cherbourg, it commanded the route down which the Germans would probably pour men and panzers once they realised that the invasion had begun. A tracer shell from the anti-aircraft guns that had fired on the pathfinders set fire to a house on the edge of the church square and at about 1.00 am the mayor called for the villagers to form a line to pass buckets of water to put the fire out. As there was a curfew in force, German soldiers from the garrison came out to oversee the operation. To everyone's astonishment as they were putting the fire out, the drone of more aircraft was heard overhead. American paratroopers, again thrown off position, began coming down – some of them right into the main square. A series of extraordinary incidents, highlighted in the feature film *The Longest Day*, began to unfold. One paratrooper after another was blown by the strong winds into the main square and the German soldiers running about below opened fire on them. Laden with ammunition and grenades, some paratroopers hit by German bullets simply blew up. Others landed in trees and before they could cut themselves free were fired on by the Germans with their automatic weapons. The most unlucky ones were drawn by the winds right into the fire itself. The parachute of one paratrooper, Private John Steele, got caught on the steeple of the church tower and he hung there, suspended by his harness, watching the mayhem below. Remarkably he survived to tell the tale with only an injured foot, and some time later he was taken prisoner. To those present, it seemed as though the centre of the Allied assault was the main square of this small village. In fact probably no more than twenty American paratroopers had landed in the village, and of these about half had been killed.

St Mère Église today acts as a sort of pilgrimage centre for American paratroop veterans visiting Normandy. Its popular Museum features a C-47 in the colours it would have worn for the most famous night drop in history.

they began to round up more soldiers. Bizarrely, most of them were officers and within an hour Taylor had a group around him consisting of two generals, four colonels, four lieutenants, several NCOs and a dozen or so privates. 'Never in the annals of warfare,' quipped General Taylor, 'have so few been commanded by so many!'

The Germans were thoroughly confused by the reports that were now coming in of paratroop drops over such a wide vicinity. Adding to this confusion were reports of dummy paratroops that had been dropped by two SAS teams, miles to the east near Le Havre. The Germans could make no sense of these varied sightings. And now, as the paratroopers got to work, their first action was to cut communication wires and to blow-up telephone poles wherever they saw them. Aided by intelligence from the French resistance, one group of paras headed for a top secret underground German communication centre which they succeeded in destroying. This added to the German confusion and left countless German garrisons cut off without any information on what was happening as the night progressed. Added to this, the Allies were lucky that the Germans were conducting a major map exercise in Rennes and several senior officers were absent at this. Rommel was also away from the action, visiting his wife on her birthday. And at the top level, Hitler had given strict instructions that none of the panzer divisions held in reserve were to be moved without specific instruction from himself. He was not to be disturbed until the morning but even then he responded slowly, believing that everything taking place in Normandy was merely a decoy to the major assault

THE GLIDER

In 1941, the American military placed orders for a series of prototype gliders. The Waco design was chosen and went into production. Eventually almost fourteen thousand were built and they played a vital role in the Allied victories later in the war. The Waco could carry 15 fully armed troops, or a jeep and its crew, or a small field gun. It was towed to its objective, then released, to attempt a controlled landing, which often ended as more of a crash-landing.

The British favoured the slightly larger Horsa glider, made of plywood and fabric, which carried 25 soldiers. On landing its undercarriage would sometimes shear off and it would land on its skids. This was a dangerous time and the men inside would brace themselves by linking arms and lifting their legs up off the floor. Landing was especially hazardous for the pilots at the front who would be the first into any obstruction, like the 'Asparagus' defences, or a hedgerow or some trees.

The C-47 was the natural choice for a glider tug. Its low take-off speed and its great strength meant that it could actually tow two gliders at the same time. Two ropes of unequal length would be attached to a towing eye below the tail of the C-47. The two gliders would be hooked on and positioned on the runway, one behind the other. The C-47 would taxi forward slowly, until both ropes were taught. Under full power, the C-47 would set off down the runway and gradually first one, then the other glider would become airborne. Finally, the C-47 itself would lift off and the trio would slowly gain height. Over the landing zone, the gliders would cast off the tow and land, as best they could, in whatever open space they could find. Despite the risks, gliders proved to be a very effective means of delivering men and materials to the war zone.

that would come later in the Pas de Calais.

Meanwhile, at the other end of the planned landing zone, the British paratroopers of the 6th Airborne Division were having much better luck. They had two principal sets of objectives. Firstly, to seize and keep control of two major bridges over the Caen Canal and the Orne River. The second objective was to overpower and put out of action the heavy 150 mm gun battery at Merville, which it was thought could wreak havoc on the landings at Sword Beach nearby. Further east, more paras would land and destroy a set of bridges across the Dives River to ensure that German panzer reinforcements could not strike at the Allied beachheads.

The 6th Airborne Division had been formed in April 1943 and took on the motto 'Go to It!' Like the American paras, the 6th Airborne was an elite unit of the British Army and spent a year training for the invasion that everyone knew was coming. As the specific tasks came into focus, so different units were assigned their objectives. The 2nd Battalion of the Oxfordshire and Buckinghamshire Light Infantry was given one of the toughest tasks of all, to capture intact a bridge across the Caen Canal. The Bridge was to go down in history as Pegasus Bridge. It was known to be well defended and probably wired up with explosives to be detonated if the garrison came under attack. It was decided that this task would best be undertaken by gliderborne troops towed by Halifax bombers and C-47s from airfields in southern England. Major John Howard led D Company of the Ox and Bucks who were to lead this daring operation. They trained for the mission

by practising their assault on a bridge across the Exe canal near Exeter which was judged to be almost identical to the bridge in Normandy.

The aircraft hauling the perilously fragile Horsa gliders took off as darkness fell and flew to the exact spot over the French coast near Ouistreham where they released their gliders. The pilots of the gliders then had the task of identifying their landing zones and to crash-land their gliders as near to their target as possible. The pilots then joined the men as active troopers in the ground operation. Staff Sergeant Jimmy Wallwork was flying the first glider with its cargo of twenty-eight men of D Company of the Ox and Bucks. In a piece of superb flying Sergeant Wallwork brought his glider down to land about 50 yards from the Bridge, crashing through the barbed wire defences, exactly as planned. Behind him two further gliders made perfect landings, both inside the 300 yard Landing Zone. This was a display of flying that was later described by the commander of the Air Forces on D-Day, Air Vice Marshall Leigh Mallory, as 'One of the most outstanding flying achievements of the Second World War.' Having landed precisely on target, the men ran forward to take the Bridge.

In another daring mission, a second group of men from the Ox and Bucks seized control of the bridge across the Orne River at Ranville. Here the sight of the airborne troops appearing silently out of the night sky made the German guards decide to run away rather than fight. Within a little more than ten minutes both bridges had been captured

PEGASUS BRIDGE

The first gliders of the Ox and Bucks silently descended towards their target and crashed through the defences around Pegasus Bridge, exactly on schedule at 00.16 hours on the morning of 6th June. The German sentries thought the sound of splintering wood and screeching metal was nothing more than distant firing during what they took to be another typical air-raid. Some of the men were temporarily knocked unconscious by the force of the landing, but within seconds Major Howard and platoon commander Lieutenant Den Brotheridge led their men out of the gliders and towards the bridge only yards away. A few seconds later a 17 year old German sentry patrolling across the bridge was astonished to see a group of black faced British airborne troops appear out of the dark, apparently from nowhere. He called out to the other sentry who fired a flair to light up the Bridge. Lieutenant Brotheridge fired from his hip unleashing a full clip of 32 rounds from his Sten gun. The sentry was killed immediately – the first man that day to die defending Hitler's Fortress Europe. The firing alerted the rest of the German garrison and as Brotheridge led his platoon racing across the bridge, some defenders on the other bank returned fire. Within minutes, the first group of men had flushed out all the defenders of the Bridge. Sappers quickly went to work to disconnect any explosives attached to the bridge. To their surprise they found none – the German commander, fearing an attack by the Resistance, had not connected the explosive charges that night. By 00.22 hours, only six minutes after landing, Major Howard had complete control of Pegasus Bridge. In a magnificent feat of arms, the first British objective of D-Day had been won. But Lieut Brotheridge who had led the first platoon across the bridge had been wounded in the neck. As the company doctor tried to treat the wound he died – the first Allied soldier to be killed by enemy fire on D-Day.

Although no longer in use, Pegasus Bridge has now been preserved as a monument to the men of 6th Airborne Division who began the liberation of France that night.

intact. The British troops could barely believe their luck and began to transmit by radio the code words 'Ham and Jam' to signify that both bridges were now in their control. About 30 minutes later, the aircraft bringing reinforcements from 5th Paratroop Brigade arrived over the scene. Some paratroopers jumped from C-47 Dakotas, as the British called them, others came in by glider, again towed by C-47s and by Halifaxes, bringing artillery and vehicles. But as with the Americans, many of these paras were blown off course or dropped in the wrong place. An hour or so later, only about one third of the anticipated force of reinforcements had arrived at Pegasus Bridge to help Major Howard cling on to his crucial objective. Like the Americans, he would face a long night ahead.

Near to the coast at Merville, aerial reconnaissance had identified a battery of 150 mm guns. With a range of eight miles they could create havoc on the nearby Sword landing beach only three miles away. 9th Paratroop Brigade led by Lieutenant Colonel Terence Otway was assigned the task of assaulting the battery. About 750 men and an array of assault equipment and explosives to destroy the guns were to be dropped for the assault. But almost everything went wrong for this operation. The C-47 pilots carrying the paras were again thrown off position by the intensity of the German anti-aircraft fire. And many of the gliders that were to bring in the heavier equipment mistook their landing zones or were damaged on landing. By 02.30 hours, only a

small part of Lieutenant Colonel Otway's assault force, about 150 men, had assembled at the rendezvous point in a nearby wood. Otway was faced with a difficult choice – whether to proceed with the attack against a well defended enemy position or abandon the operation. 'It was a question of move off or give up,' Otway later recalled. But he concluded 'In the Parachute Regiment, giving up is not an option.'

Otway led his small force in a head-on attack against the German battery. It was a frontal assault as he did not have enough men to attack from all sides, as planned. Some of his men had to advance through an uncleared minefield. The Germans defended their position from well dug-in machine gun outposts behind barbed wire defences. With gallantry and real bravery the attackers pressed home their assault. After a few minutes there was chaos and it was impossible to tell what was happening. But the well trained paras pressed forwards and eventually penetrated to the heart of the battery. There, after hand to hand fighting they took control of the gun emplacements. It was all over in twenty minutes. But to their surprise, the victorious paras found not 150 mm heavy guns, but 75 mm Czech and French guns taken out of the Maginot Line. The intelligence assessments had been wrong. Nevertheless, lacking the explosives that had gone astray with the gliders, the paras destroyed the guns with their gammon grenades, and according to the plan, withdrew. Of the 150 men in Otway's force that made the assault, barely eighty paras walked away from the

A reconnaissance photograph of the Merville Battery taken two months before D-Day.

Merville Battery. Of the 200 German defenders, most had been killed or wounded. Only twenty-two uninjured Germans were taken prisoner. It was another illustration of how effective well trained and bravely led soldiers could be, even in the most daunting of situations.

Further east, things again went horribly wrong for teams of British and Canadian paratroopers who were spread out across miles of occupied territory. Their mission was to destroy three bridges across the River Dives. One squad that managed to form-up consisted of only seven men. They commandeered a medical jeep and trailer, threw out the bottles of blood and splints, loaded it with explosives and drove right through a German garrison, eventually to reach their bridge at Troarn and blow it up. The other two bridges at Bures were also destroyed.

Through the night more reinforcements were brought in by glider, to back up the paratroopers struggling to attain or to hold on to their first objectives. In the American sector, many of these gliders came to terrible grief as they crashed into trees or hedgerows. More than one in three gliders were broken into pieces and dozens of men were killed or wounded. Many of the pilots who brought the gliders in broke their legs, or worse, on landing. Most of the equipment, guns, jeeps, even a bulldozer, was smashed and was unusable. Despite all the detailed planning that had gone into these operations, no one had really

This Horsa of the 82nd US Airborne crashed on the evening of D-Day killing eighteen men.

reckoned on the destructive power of the characteristic Norman hedgerow – a problem that would soon become a curse on the fighting in Normandy.

By the dawn of D-Day, the C-47s had completed their initial task – to drop 17,000 American and 7,000 British paratroopers behind enemy lines. During that long night, and over the next few days, it was up to these tough and determined fighters to organise themselves on landing and to fight for and hold on to their objectives, until relieved by the main landing force fighting its way inland. In the western sector, the American paras of the 82nd and 101st fought bravely for weeks to come. At St Mère Église, where some of the paras had been shot to pieces as they came down, the German garrison, remarkably, went back to bed after this action at about 2.00 am. A group of about 180 paras succeeded in taking this key objective before dawn. This time the German garrison surrendered without much of a fight to the fearsome looking Americans. And the citizens of St Mère Église woke up to find their village in American hands – the first French community to be liberated by the Allies.

Elsewhere, the American paras were not so successful. Many of the paratroopers were still struggling to regroup and find their units. Most of them were operating, if at all, in small, isolated units. Even twenty-fours later, only about 2,500 of the 6,000 men of the 101st who had been dropped, had assembled in organised units. Much of their equipment had been destroyed or was lost in the drop. Without heavy weapons they were severely weakened and perhaps worst of all, so many radios had been smashed that most of the paras had no means by which to contact others. Much of the night was lost in trying to assemble and

SNATCHING UP GLIDERS

One of the most extraordinary tasks the C-47 ever performed was the gathering up of gliders from the ground where it was not possible for the C-47 to land. The glider was usually treated as expendable. Its low cost, when compared to a powered aircraft, meant that its one trip was regarded as an economic proposition. But, as the number of glider-borne operations increased, so did the need to recover and re-use them. The possibility of snatching them off the ground was investigated. Yet again, the C-47 proved a master of the task. Given an unobstructed take-off run for the glider, the looped end of its tow rope could be suspended between two poles and caught by a low-flying C-47, trailing a long hook on a cable.

locate precisely where they were. The key bridges over the Douve River were not captured and the causeways across the flooded Merderet had not been secured. But small units fought tenaciously. In a host of separate, small-scale skirmishes, groups of paratroopers kept the Germans back. Bob Murphy, one of the first pathfinders to land who had so terrified the schoolmistress in her garden, went on to take part in a heroic action at la Fiére bridge over the Merderet. With only three men and a couple of bazooka anti-tank weapons, they held off an attack by three panzers all of which were put out of action. The tanks did not pass. And the men on Utah Beach were safe.

Almost everywhere, the Germans were confused by the night airborne assault and failed to react effectively. Colonel Hans von Luck commanded the 125th Regiment of the 21st Panzer Division – the unit which Rommel relied on, to the east of Caen, to throw the Allies back into the sea. Despite the confusion of the reports coming in, von Luck roused his men and by 2.30 am they were fully mobilised, lined up by their vehicles, with engines running and ready to go. But only Hitler could give the order for the panzers to move – and he was asleep. Gerd von Rundstedt, Commander in Chief of Army Group West was also asleep and was not woken. Rommel was away with his wife. Struggling to interpret the disparate accounts of the paratroop landings, the headquarters of Army Group West concluded 'We are not confronted by a major action.' The paratroopers on the ground were fortunate. Von Luck and his tanks, had they been ordered into action, would have headed straight for the Orne River and canal

Men of the 101st US Airborne Division check houses on the east side of the town of Carentan four days after D-Day.

bridges where Major Howard was holding on with virtually no anti-tank weapons since most had been lost in the glider crashes.

But the overall objectives of the airborne mission had been achieved. They had caused enough confusion to prevent the enemy from counter-attacking in force against the seaborne invasion on the following morning. But lessons had to be learned. At a post mortem of the airborne assault back in England in August 1944, it was requested that the C-47 pilots should be better trained in flying through anti-aircraft fire and instructed that wild evasive action was pointless in avoiding the flak. Also, it was decided that maintaining radio silence was counter-productive and prevented vital communication between the pilots. Better plans for assembly of the paras on the ground were made. More radio sets were to be dropped and equipment was to be secured better to survive the drop. The American paratroopers decided to adopt the quick release mechanism used by the British paratroopers to get out of their harnesses more quickly.

Improvements in tactics and equipment had to be made, but the plane that had flown the men behind the enemy lines never came under criticism. Even when hit, the C-47s had flown on. Only twenty aircraft out of the 900 that had flown that night failed to return. And after the night operation was finished they started again, bringing over more vital supplies. As soon as rough landing strips could be improvised the C-47s came in to fly out the wounded. Many an injured

Yet another role for the ubiquitous C-47 – the speedy evacuation of wounded from the war zone to a hospital back in England.

GI or a British Tommy owed his life to a C-47 acting as an air ambulance, flying him from a field hospital back to England for proper medical care. For weeks to come the C-47s kept up an endless two-way shuttle, bringing supplies in and evacuating the wounded out of the growing beachhead. The C-47 had earned its battle honours as the workhorse that made possible the paratroop drop before D-day and the accumulation of supplies afterwards. And every C-47 flew unarmed through dangerous skies.

For the rest of the war, the C-47 was never far behind the advancing front line. In Operation Market Garden in September, the RAF Dakotas once again launched a huge paratroop drop behind enemy lines. This time the strategy did not work and the paras trying to seize vital bridges over the Rhine were stranded – on a bridge too far. Through the winter of 1944 and the spring of 1945, American and British C-47s flew tens of thousands of sorties to keep the momentum of the advance going. And ever more ingenious tasks were invented for the multi-purpose flying workhorse.

When the war ended, thousands of aircraft became redundant overnight. Brand new, four-engined bombers, which had cost the American taxpayer a small fortune to build, were flown straight from the factory to storage sites. Soon they were being sold off to scrap merchants, often for less than the value of the fuel in their tanks. Most of the fighters went the same way but, for the C-47, it was a very different story. For as little as $2,000, an ex-army pilot could buy a C-47 at a government sale and set up in business. Some went on hauling freight, others fitted passenger seats and interior trim, to create a very

THE BERLIN AIRLIFT

In the years following the end of the Second World War, the former Allies began to fall out – for both ideological and territorial reasons. Europe divided into two rival camps in this new Cold War with an 'iron curtain' down the middle. Many of the tensions of the Cold War focused on the city of Berlin, well inside the Soviet zone of the military occupation of Germany, but itself jointly occupied by the Americans, British, French and Soviets. In June 1948, Stalin ordered a blockade of Berlin to try to force the west to withdraw from the city. As the western leaders struggled to respond, a general who had been part of the campaign to fly supplies into China over the 'hump' during the war suggested an airlift. Once again the C-47 came to the rescue and 80 of them began to fly crucial supplies of food, coal, petrol, potatoes and medical supplies from bases in western Germany into the beleagured city of Berlin. But with a payload of 3 tons, it seemed an impossible task to meet the daily requirement of up to 12,000 tons of supplies. However, the airlift continued and gangs of workers eventually learned to unload an aircraft in Berlin in just 7 minutes. The C-47s would then turn around and return with a second load, later in the day.

During the Berlin airlift, the C-47 was eclipsed by the C-54 Skymaster with a payload of 9 tons and then by the huge C-74 Globemaster, a freight version of the Superfortress bomber, which could carry in up to 23 tons of supplies. At the airlift's peak, flights arrived at the airfields of west Berlin every 90 seconds. The airlift kept Berlin going through the winter of 1948-9 and in one day in April 1949, a record number of nearly 1400 flights brought an extraordinary 13,000 tons of supplies into the city. The airlift convinced Stalin that he could not win and in May 1949 the Soviet blockade was lifted.

The Allied air forces that had once dropped tons of bombs on Berlin daily now helped to keep the city alive, bringing in food and fuel. And, of course, the C-47 was inevitably the plane that got the airlift going.

basic version of the pre war DC-3 airliner. By squeezing in another row of seats, 28 passengers could be accommodated in reasonable comfort, though the central gangway was barely wide enough. The big airlines got back many of their DC-3s, which had been commandeered by the military, and restored them to their original condition. They also made strenuous efforts to drive the small independent operators out of business. But often the small outfits were providing a service which the bigger airlines couldn't offer, at a price they couldn't match.

Because the C-47 was not classed as a weapon, there were few restrictions on its sale to governments around the world. At least 50 air forces are known to have operated the type and it played a leading role in many small wars. It also took part in some very big ones. In Korea and Vietnam, C-47s were still found to be the best tool for the job of battlefield transport. In Vietnam, they took on an untypically aggressive role. C-47s were fitted with three enormous machine guns, mounted to fire from the doorway and the two rear-most windows on the left side. Flying in a tight circle at about three thousand feet, banked at 30 degrees, the aircraft could saturate a ground target with 18,000 rounds a minute. Each carried a ton of ammunition. Donald Douglas and his team could never have imagined such a ferocious role for their docile airliner.

As the big airlines got back to work after the war, they soon began

When the war ended a great many C-47s became available for re-employment in the role for which they were originally designed. Two DC-3s, in the service of British European Airways, load up at Northolt Airport in 1949.

to replace their ageing DC-3s with bigger aircraft. But this simply released more for low-cost charter and freight work. In the late 1940s and early 1950s, the American authorities made several attempts to ground the type, mostly at the urging of the big operators, who disliked the competition, and of the aircraft builders, who wanted new sales. But since it could never be proved that the DC-3 was becoming unsafe, and since so many were still in service, it was finally accepted as indestructible and allowed to continue indefinitely. Today there are DC-3s, mostly ex-military C-47s, still earning their living. Many have now spent more than ten years of their life in the air. Thanks to the low stresses produced in the airframe, they can still fly safely, long after their intended replacements have gone to the breakers. Because their engines are a reliable, air-cooled design, built in huge numbers during the war, they rarely break down and spares are still available. Surprisingly, the main problem for DC-3 operators today is not the age of the aircraft, but lack of suitable fuel. Most commercial aircraft are now powered by jets, or turbo-props which use jet fuel. Large supplies of 'Avgas', the high octane fuel for piston engines, are becoming harder to find.

One solution is to re-fit the DC-3 with modern, turbo-prop engines. But the cost is high and for most operators the investment would be uneconomic. The surviving DC-3s are mostly in service in the Third World. Often they fly in extreme conditions which would not suit the more sophisticated modern engines. A dust storm or tropical downpour, which could play havoc with an electronic control system, will usually have little effect on a DC-3. They have probably been worked even harder in their post war roles than they were in combat. Maintenance is often neglected and they are frequently overloaded. In 1949, a C-47 is known to have carried 93 victims of a Bolivian earthquake to safety – many were small children, but it's still an extraordinary feat for an aircraft which began life as a 21 seat airliner.

In the developed world, companies like Air Atlantique, based at Coventry in England, still find the type economic to fly as an ad-hoc freight carrier. They operate a fleet of ex military C-47s which have passed through several owners. Some have served as passenger carriers, but all still retain their large loading doors. One was a veteran of the Berlin airlift and still had traces of coal dust beneath the floor when Air Atlantique engineers inspected it. A newer, more expensive aircraft would have to be kept fully employed, to justify the investment. But, thanks to their low initial cost and their reliability, the C-47s can be kept on stand-by for long periods waiting for short notice charter work. When the phone rings and an urgent consignment of car components has to be sent across Europe, they can be in the air in less than an hour. Some of the fleet are committed to a long-term, anti-pollution contract with the British Government. Fitted with chemical tanks and spraying equipment, their mission is to disperse oil spills around the coast of Britain. Like the lifeboat service, they may spend most of their time waiting for the call to action, but when it comes, the public expects them to be there. The stirring sight of a wartime C-47 on a low-level mission is recreated once more, even if today's enemy is an oil slick.

Unlike the Spitfire, the DC-3 was not the product of a single individual's vision. It grew, not from a flash of inspiration, but from a group of practical engineers working together and a process of development and evolution. The story of its birth is far less romantic than the birth of the Spitfire, but the end result is similar. Both processes produced brilliant designs, which worked and went on working. But while the Spitfire evolved, under the pressure of competition, into an aircraft which had doubled in power and almost doubled in weight by the end of its development, the basic DC-3 hardly changed at all.

It is a tribute to the Douglas design team that they managed to get almost everything right on the DC-3. After the war there were many attempts to develop a successor to the original design. Long haul

A Royal New Zealand Air Force Dakota in operation against Malayan terrorists. Dakotas were finally retired from the RNZAF in 1977 after thirty-four years faithful service.

aircraft grew bigger and faster, but the need for a twin engine, medium range, low cost transport remained and many manufacturers attempted to capture the market. But nothing managed to displace the DC-3. None of the newer aircraft managed to combine all the same qualities in one machine. They were either too easily damaged by rough handling, or too prone to mechanical failure, or too expensive to buy and operate.

There are other aircraft which might challenge the DC-3/C-47 design for the 'Greatest Ever' title. Military types may seem the obvious choice. They help to make history, like the British Spitfire, or soldier on year after year, like the American B52 bomber, but their job is to destroy the enemy, not to create lasting social revolutions. That is the work of civil air transport. The only serious rivals to the DC-3 are both Boeing designs, the company whose pioneering 247 was eclipsed by Douglas in the 1930s. The Boeing 707 of the 1950s was the first jet airliner to take the industry by storm, following the commercial failure of the pioneering British Comet. It sold to almost every airline across the world and can still be found, downgraded to freight duties. Its natural successor was another triumph for Boeing – the 747 Jumbo Jet. With far more seats and lower operating costs, it boosted the profitability of the long haul airlines and widened the appeal of air travel still further. But both the Boeings were simply spreading the gospel according to Donald Douglas. They increased the capacity,

This civil Super DC-3 found no customers among the airlines and attempts were made to sell it to the USAF when it was designated YC-47F. It was handed over to the US Navy. Here the YC-47 is being boosted into the air by solid-fuel rockets – JATO. These gave it short field take-off capability.

range and economy of flight, but it was the DC-3 which laid the foundations.

Even without its wartime role, the DC-3 would have to be credited with transforming the business of transporting passengers by air. The fact that it then not only went to war, but became one of the most versatile and effective weapons ever devised makes it unique. The huge size of the wartime fleet dwarfs the production figures for civil airliners and ensured the survival of large numbers into the post war era. The fact that the survivors were then able to launch yet another revolution in world wide air travel, is impressive. While the fact that, in the 21st Century, many are still at work, is nothing short of incredible. The millions who now think nothing of going by air have good reason to thank Donald Douglas. It is ironic that the company which bears his name, has now been swallowed by its old rival – Boeing. Douglas went on to build many other successful aircraft, but his finest monument remains the DC-3. Before his death in 1981 he wrote:

> *'I don't believe that any of us who worked on the design and development quite realised we were building an aeroplane that would outlast the careers of all of us. Perhaps she will fly on forever, I hope she does'.*

Chapter Five

SHERMAN ASSAULT

15 September 1916, was a momentous day in the history of warfare. At dawn on that day a new weapon of war had its baptism of fire. The British army used tanks for the first time in an attempt to break through the enemy lines in the Battle of the Somme and to speed up that deadly offensive which had already raged for two and a half terrible months. The machine gun had reduced warfare to a stalemate in which the armies of industrial nations could do no more than face each other across no-man's land from well dug-in defences. Two lines of trenches snaked across Europe from the Channel to the Alps. And between the trenches of the Western Front lay an immense mass of barbed wire. The only way either side took the offensive was through human-wave assaults which involved massive loss of life. The tank was a mighty monster developed as an antidote to the machine gun and to barbed wire.

Many have claimed to be 'inventor' of the tank and the origins of this war machine have been discussed at length on many occasions. Suffice it to say here that the invention of the tank was as much a

The British invention that would introduce a new aspect to warfare of the twentieth century. This dramatic view of a MkI gives some idea of what it must have been like for the German infantry on the receiving end.

British contribution towards warfare as the machine gun had been an American contribution through its inventor, Hiram Maxim. The first detailed plans were laid in 1915 at the Admiralty with the encouragement of Winston Churchill, then First Lord of the Admiralty. At this stage the devices were known as 'landships'. But soon a remarkably cautious and unenthusiastic army was persuaded to take the machine over and after trials in February 1916, a unit called The Heavy Section of the Machine Gun Corps began training at Thetford in Norfolk with the new vehicles. In addition to armour plating to protect the vehicles from shell and machine gun fire, they were equipped with tracks – as wheels were not sufficient to carry the machine forward through the shell holes and the wire of the Western Front. A brilliant team of engineers developed the design of this entirely new type of tracked vehicle. To maintain total secrecy a name had to be invented to avoid news of the machine getting out, whilst providing a plausible description for anyone who saw the tarpaulined device in transit. Various words were considered including 'cistern' and 'reservoir', but fortunately neither of these were chosen and the enigmatic word 'tank' was finally settled upon.

Against the advice of those who had developed the tank, the machines were first hurriedly thrown into the next phase of the Somme offensive in September 1916. Only sixty of the 150 tanks ordered had yet arrived in France. Of these only thirty-two made it to

The new wonder weapon which, it was hoped, would bring an end to the stalemate on the Western Front. How best to use the new invention was learned the hard way through grim experience.

the starting line. After a three day bombardment had churned the Somme battlefield into a cratered quagmire, nine more tanks broke down and a further five were stranded in shell craters and abandoned. But the remaining tanks, although small in number, succeeded in breaking through the barbed wire defences and caused panic in the enemy. A German regimental history vividly describes their impact:

> *'The arrival of the tanks on the scene had the most shattering effect on the men. They felt quite powerless against these monsters which crawled along the top of the trench enfilading it with continuous machine gun fire...'*

Although successful in achieving their first day objectives, the German line elsewhere along the Somme held and the tanks did not bring about the anticipated breakthrough. Too few tanks had been used; tactics for their deployment had not been developed; commanders and men had not worked out how best to take advantage of them. And, of course, the surprise effect of their first use had been squandered.

In November 1917 at Cambrai, tanks nearly achieved the total breakthrough they had been designed for. With no preliminary bombardment, a large body of tanks smashed through the German lines causing terror amongst the enemy. The tanks tore a hole in the German line four miles wide. At one point the tanks advanced five miles and emerged into open country. With minimal casualties, the army won more ground in a day than in three months of slaughter in

Infantry practising advancing with tanks, in 1917. At the Battle of Cambrai in November 1917, the new tactics paid off and a four-mile break in the German Line was accomplished.

the battle of Passchendaele. But the British High Command was paralysed by this unexpected success and failed to take advantage of it. There was no infantry available after the losses in Flanders and the cavalry were mowed down by the surviving machine gunners. The Germans threw reserve divisions at the gap and soon the line was almost back to where it had started. Another great advantage had been thrown away.

In the summer and autumn offensives of 1918 tanks were again used extensively. General Ludendorff called August 8th, 1918 'the black day of the German army' adding that 'mass attacks by tanks...remained hereafter our most dangerous enemies.' Other German generals realised the importance of the tank in what now led up to their final defeat. 'It was not the genius of General Foch that beat us' wrote one 'but 'General Tank'.' However, beset by mechanical problems which often gave them a bad reputation, the tanks left most British generals unimpressed. Haig called the tanks a 'minor factor' in victory. By the end of the war the British High Command concluded they were a nine-day wonder. And in the United States, the Tank Corps was disbanded in 1919.

During the late 1920s and '30s, progressive military thinking revolved around concepts of mobile, mechanised war. Although the most senior commanders of the British army lived in a world hidebound by tradition, there was debate about new ideas amongst

The French Renault FT 17 Tank saw service in the Great War in 1917 and was still in use in 1939. The British soldier standing alongside gives an indication of the cramped conditions in this diminutive fighting machine.

younger, junior officers. Two British military thinkers, J. C. Fuller and Basil Liddell Hart laid down the theoretical basis for a new style of armoured warfare. Their ideas ushered in a period of experimentation with armoured vehicles in the early 1930s which put the British army ahead of the world. But financial cutbacks and the overwhelming force of tradition caused these developments to be abandoned. The new ideas however were taken up by German military strategists, men like Heinz Guderian, who developed a whole new theory of what became known as 'lightning war' – *Blitzkrieg*. In 1935, the German army included three armoured panzer divisions; by 1939, there were six and by 1940, ten.

This military strategy was displayed at its best in May 1940, when the Germans launched their offensive against France, Belgium and the Netherlands. Fast moving tank units backed by infantry were at the heart of the assault. After paratroopers seized key objectives, nine panzer divisions broke through in the Ardennes forest and in only three days reached the river Meuse. Each panzer division consisted of infantry, artillery and engineers, working closely together as a combined unit with excellent communications, under a leadership that believed in flexibility and initiative. After bitter fighting, the panzer divisions crossed the river Meuse and broke through into open country. The 'race to the Channel' was on. The panzers advanced at an average of 20-25 miles a day, with their infantry transported in trucks following them up. Often they ignored the conventional need for flank protection as long as the forward momentum could be kept up. Ten days after the offensive had begun, Guderian's panzers reached the

KEY CONCEPTS OF TANK DESIGN

The tank is effectively a mobile fortification. Its basic elements are the hull, the turret and the tracks. The hull is the main body of the machine, containing the engine, drive mechanism, fuel and ammunition. On top of this is mounted a rotating turret, containing the gun. On each side of the hull, caterpillar tracks carry the machine and move it forward.

To be successful in combat, the tank needs three ingredients: maximum firepower, maximum protective armour and maximum mobility. But, as with most mechanical designs, these elements tend to conflict and any design must be a compromise. Maximum firepower means a large gun, with a large turret to accommodate it. This in turn means a large hull to carry the turret. The combination makes the tank a bigger target and increases the area of armour plate required for protection. But as its weight increases, the tank's mobility decreases. It needs larger tracks to spread the load on soft ground and a bigger engine with a stronger drive train, which again add weight. The result can be a machine which is vulnerable to attack, despite its firepower, because it is too slow and unwieldy.

The World War One tank was heavy, cumbersome and agonisingly slow. Between the wars, the light tank became popular because of its speed and mobility. But its thin armour and small-calibre gun proved to be useless against heavy weapons and the trend during World War Two was towards ever increasing firepower, thicker armour and extra weight. This required complex systems to rotate the heavy turret and elevate the gun. By the end of the war, monsters had been developed which weighed over 60 tons, with 600hp engines, 150mm armour and guns of up to 128mm calibre. But the tank was essentially a machine intended for offensive action, replacing the cavalry. And the Allied tank designers tended to put greater emphasis on speed and mobility than on heaviness and the thickness of armour plating.

coast at Abbeville – on the same day that Brussells fell to the Germans. The French army's key defensive shield, the Maginot Line had been all but bypassed. The Allied armies succeeded in withdrawing from Dunkirk only after the panzers had been ordered to halt their advance at Boulogne. It took the Germans only three weeks to smash the Allies. The effective use of panzers, backed up with infantry and engineers in a well orchestrated combined operation, was what blitzkrieg was all about – and proved the key to German victory.

Meanwhile, in the United States political and military leaders watched events in Europe with alarm. The United States Army was in a poor state – it was tiny and equipped with only a few hundred tanks mostly of World War One vintage. The Tank Corps had been disbanded after the First World War and, astonishingly, only thirty-five tanks had been built in the US between 1920 and 1935! Even more alarming was the fact that the firepower of the German panzers had made almost every tank in the US arsenal obsolete overnight. There was nothing in the United States to match the German vehicles. The press expressed outrage at America's unpreparedness and the Senate took up the theme. Something had to be done – and quickly.

Although still only neutral, on 30 June 1940, a National Munitions Program was rapidly drawn up to coordinate America's rearmament. At the forefront of this would be the production of tanks. With remarkable vision the production target rate was set at the then

Czech-built 38t panzers during the invasion of France in May 1940. French colonial troops are seen surrendering to the German forces.

General Adna R. Chaffee

seemingly incredible level of one thousand new tanks each month. Ten days later, a new Armored Force was created under General Adna R. Chaffee to take over responsibility for tanks from the infantry and cavalry. Two new armored divisions were formed. The 2nd Armored Division was to be commanded by one of the few US commanders who had experience of tank warfare from the Tank Corps in France at the end of World War One. His name was General George S. Patton.

The original plan for the increase of tank production was that heavy engineering plants across the United States would be commandeered to build tanks. However, these plans were soon abandoned. The National Defense Advisory Commission was created with leading industrialists to advise on the Munitions Program. William S. Knudsen, President of General Motors was a leading member of the Commission and he felt that the use of heavy engineering plants accustomed to the 'tailor made' construction of locomotives or cranes would not be sufficient. He argued that the only way to achieve the required level of output was for the automobile industry to turn over its management, manpower and mass-production expertise to tank production. Detroit had to be mobilised for war.

The President of the Chrysler Corporation, K. T. Keller, responded to the call. Chrysler had been founded in 1925 and was the second largest auto production company in the US. Now Keller sent a team of engineers to collect the mountain of blueprints for the existing range

A pre-war US tank design – the M2. The six-wheel suspension, with star-shaped forward drive sprocket, is an established part of the design and would remain, with some modifications, throughout wartime production.

of tanks from the government Arsenal. They weighed 186 lbs. The first plans and costings were done. But most of the existing car factories in Detroit were needed for the production of other military vehicles like trucks. Keller asked 'Why don't you have a Tank Arsenal?' and as the need was so urgent the National Munitions Program agreed. The cost of building a tank factory was estimated at $21 million. Within a month the government gave Chrysler the go-ahead and construction began on a new factory in Detroit dedicated to producing tanks. This would become famous as the Detroit Arsenal.

Things were now moving quickly. First onto the production line was intended to be the M2 Light tank. But this tank had a 37 mm gun, 25 mm armour plating and weighing in at 12 tons, had a maximum speed of 25 mph. It was already outgunned by the panzers with their 75 mm guns and heavier armour. The army planners called for a bigger gun – at least 75 mm – to match the German panzers. A weapon of this calibre was too big to be mounted in the turret of the existing tanks. So in the space of 60 days a new model was designed with the bigger gun in the hull. 10,000 working drawings were needed for its production. The order for the M2s was cancelled and replaced by orders for this new version, known as the M3 Medium Tank. By early 1941, when the Detroit Arsenal was ready to go into production, plans for the M3 were complete. But going straight from the drawing board into production led to endless problems. Production of many of the components could not keep up. Some of the first M3s off the production line went into service without the 75 mm gun. However, more than 6,000 were built over the next two years.

Different versions of the M3 were known as the Grant or the Lee.

THE DETROIT ARSENAL

In August 1940 the decision to build a Tank Arsenal in Detroit was made and a letter of intent was issued to the Chrysler Corporation to produce 1000 tanks by August 1942. The American government acquired 113 acres of farming land in Warren township 17 miles from downtown Detroit, which it leased to Chrysler. Ground was broken on 9th September 1940, and on 11 April 1941, the first tank was driven off the assembly line. In September 1941, Chrysler was asked to expand production to 750 tanks per month – a huge increase. To achieve this, in December the Chrysler plant went into production 24 hours a day, 6 days a week. The

workforce reached a total of 5,000 in August 1942, working on three assembly lines. This increased to five assembly lines by June 1944. On each assembly line the growing shell of the tank moved from station to station at fixed intervals of time. At each station an operation was completed – the installation of the engine or the mounting of the gun. Each station held a bank of parts, replenished by an overhead trolley from the stores. The whole assembly line moved forward after the fixed amount of time had elapsed – meaning that at the end of the line a completed tank was driven away for testing at each move. The complexity of supplying and feeding these assembly lines with thousands of tons of spare parts was an awesome undertaking. By December 1945, the Detroit Arsenal had produced 25,059 armoured vehicles, comprising 12 different types of heavy and medium tank from 23 to 65 tons.

Grants were supplied to the British under Lend Lease and fought in the North African desert war. Their first action was at the battle of Gazala in May 1942 and they provided the backbone of the tank forces at the Battle of El Alamein later that year. A small number were also used by the US army in the Torch landings in Tunisia in November 1942. The rest were mostly used for training. Up until this point, the lighter British tanks had been at a major disadvantage against the heavier German tanks with their superior firepower. In November 1942, General Montgomery, who led the Eighth Army in their victory at El Alamein, cabled the War Office with a cryptic tank request 'The 75 mm gun is all we require.' This seemed to endorse the view that the 75 mm weapon would suffice in future tank warfare with the Germans.

However, the M3 was always seen as an interim model and as it went into production, another team of designers began working on plans for a new tank. Civilian engineers from the US auto industry worked alongside military engineers from the US Ordnance Dept. A small contingent of British engineers and planners were also on hand to advise and comment. One wit commented that 'The Battle of Waterloo may have been won on the playing fields of Eton but this war will be won on the drawing boards of Detroit.'

The new tank design adopted a turret with a 360 degree traverse and a gyro-stabiliser designed by Westinghouse – so its gun could be

M3 Grants were the first American tanks to go into action against the German Afrika Korps at Gazala in 1942. The British Eighth Army made good use of them at El Alamein. Here some Grants move along a partly submerged road in North Africa after a flash-flood. Note the 75 mm gun in the hull not the turret.

aimed and fired, as from a ship at sea, whilst the tank was in motion. This new tank would use the same chassis and mechanical layout as the M3 with a turtle shaped cast hull, but it would have thicker 60 mm steel armour plating. Because the front of the tank was angled, the 60 mm armour plating would in effect present a thicker plate to an incoming shell. There were to be access doors at the sides and two .30 calibre machine guns fixed at the front. During trials at the Aberdeen Proving Ground in Maryland, the side doors were removed, giving a stronger structure and simplified casting. As a substitute, a second hatch was fitted above the assistant driver's station and a belly escape hatch was added. In October 1941, this new tank was put into production. Officially it was known as the M4, but following the custom of naming tanks after Civil War generals, the M4 would most often be known as the Sherman.

By the summer of 1942, all the factories producing the M3 had switched to production of the M4. The body of the Sherman came in two types. There were those with a one-piece cast steel hull. But production of this posed problems in all but the largest engineering plants so a simpler box-like, more angular welded hull was designed for those plants which lacked a major casting capability. This enabled the tank to be produced in ever greater numbers. The Sherman weighed 32 tons when fully armed and equipped. There were many

On this page and opposite are examples of the two production methods used in the construction of the Sherman: below, the bolting and welding method can be seen in the two prominent flanges on the lower section; right, the one -piece cast steel hull.

variations of the engines used by the Sherman. In the early days General Motors provided a diesel engine, Chrysler produced a multibank engine and Continental produced the air-cooled C-1 engine. But in time the highly efficient Ford V-8 cylinder petrol engine became the standard used to power the Sherman, giving a maximum speed of about 26 mph.

There was continuing debate about the firepower of the Sherman's main weapon, the 75 mm high velocity gun. Despite Montgomery's approval of the 75 mm, as the war advanced the British repeatedly argued that a superior weapon was needed and came up with their own 17-pounder. The Americans refused to fit this as standard, the British planners in Detroit later claiming simply because it was British – or NIH 'Not Invented Here'. However, some later variations of the Sherman replaced the 75 mm gun with a heavier 76 mm or 105 mm weapon. And the British Army adapted some of its Shermans to fire the long 17-pounder gun. They were called the Sherman Firefly.

The first Shermans came off the production line in July 1942 and were shipped straight into service. Some of them fought with the Eighth Army at the second battle of El Alamein in North Africa. The arrival of the Sherman made the M3 Lees and Grants obsolete. They were replaced as quickly as possible with Shermans and so a huge number were required. By the end of the war, an incredible 48,000 Shermans had rolled off the production lines – double the number of all the German tanks produced in the war. Shermans would be used not only by the US Army but were supplied in large numbers to the

PRODUCTION OF THE M4 SHERMAN

Each Sherman tank consisted of 4,537 individual parts. Of these, 1,269 were manufactured by Chrysler at the Detroit Arsenal or at one of its many other plants. The remaining 3,268 parts were produced by sub-contractors. At one period of the war, Chrysler was signing up 450 new sub-contractors each month. Eventually, Chrysler worked with more than 8,000 subcontractors in 856 cities. Many of these were small workshops whose expertise was brought into the war effort. In addition to Chrysler's Detroit Arsenal, tanks were also produced on the assembly lines of the Ford Motor Company. And a second purpose-built factory was constructed by Fisher Body at Grand Blanc, Michigan. Although there were many times when delays held up production, the overall management of this supply chain was a triumph of wartime manufacturing.

The price for the first tanks produced by Chrysler was fixed at $33,500 per tank – although a clause in the contract allowed for the rising costs of labour and supplies. In peacetime, the average number of women employed in the auto industry had been 16%. This rose to 31% during the war but peaked as high as 65% in some plants. By December 1943, the average weekly wage in the auto industry's wartime factories was $57 for men and $43 for women.

The Chrysler Corporation was appointed by the US government as the general contractor for the Sherman ,because of its ability to master the complexities of mass production and to produce at a good price – an expertise built up during two decades of ruthless competition in the auto industry prior to the outbreak of war. And it is an extraordinary tribute to the American auto industry that the cut-throat competition between the 'Big Three' of Chrysler, Ford and General Motors was entirely put on one side for the duration in order that everything should be done to contribute to victory in the war effort.

British, and later the French and the Poles; and several thousand were also supplied to the Soviet Union. The Indian, South African, Australian, New Zealand and Chinese armies also all fought with Shermans.

Fast, manoeuvrable and reliable, the Sherman tank was well suited to offensive armoured warfare. The design also made the tank easy to service and good to drive. Later versions of the Sherman could go for 400 hours before the engine needed maintenance. The precision of the auto industry's assembly lines made them remarkably dependable for the rugged conditions in which they were used. However, the Sherman had several major drawbacks. It lacked the firepower of the German tanks which could outgun it any day. And its armour plating was thinner than that of the enemy tanks – which would have real consequences later on the battlefield. Also, because of its narrow base, stemming from the days when the width of the tank was limited by the width of army pontoon bridges, the Sherman was relatively high above ground. This would prove a problem in the hedgerows of Normandy. But American mass-production meant that the Sherman became available in vast numbers. It was never intended to be the best tank in the field – but it was hoped that by overwhelming force of numbers it could help to forge victory on the anvil of battle.

Each Sherman was operated by a crew of five. The tank commander was stationed in the rear of the turret and would stand up and look out from above the hatch when the tank was not under fire. The gunner was placed almost in front of the commander, his eye close to the

CHURCHILL GETS VITAL SHERMANS

The first Sherman tanks were just about to start rolling off the Detroit assembly line when Winston Churchill happened to be in Washington staying at the White House. Whilst he was there, on 20 June 1942, the devastating news came through of the fall of Tobruk, which the Prime Minister regarded as a humiliation and one of the heaviest blows of the war. President Roosevelt seeing the shock of this news on his British ally asked 'What can we do to help?' Churchill immediately replied 'Give us as many Sherman tanks as you can spare, and ship them to the Middle East as quickly as possible.' Roosevelt called for General Marshall who arrived within minutes. He pointed out that the first tanks had been allocated to US Armored Divisions but immediately agreed to the Prime Minister's request. Three hundred Sherman tanks were despatched in America's fastest ships to Suez where some of them experienced the Sherman's baptism of fire at the Battle of El Alamein. Rommel wrote after the battle 'Their new tank, the General Sherman, which came into action for the first time during this battle, showed itself superior to any of ours.' The battle of El Alamein proved to be a turning point in the Second World War.

rubber-padded telescopic sights. The loader sat to his left – and he also tuned the radio for communication with the rest of the unit. The driver sat in the left bow of the tank – his assistant in the right bow also operated the front machine gun. All of the crew had persicopes to see out and additionally the two drivers could raise their seats to see out above the hatches. Every Sherman had a radio for external contact and an interphone system for crew communication. Steering was by levers which operated brakes on either side – to slow down both levers were pulled back at once.

The crews would find the Sherman relatively spacious after earlier tanks but they could be desperately dangerous. A hit by a high-velocity shell could cause an instant explosion. If it penetrated the armour, by ricocheting inside the steel structure it could cause dreadful carnage of both metal and flesh. If the ammunition or fuel was ignited then the tank went up in flames in an instant, and for all the crew members the only escape was to get out quickly from a nearby hatch. Crews estimated they had no more than a few seconds to escape from a Sherman if it had been hit. Thick black smoke would pour out of the turret alternating with intense flame in a terrifying jet built up within the confines of the steel hull. The British graphically described it as 'brewing-up'. More cruelly the Shermans were sometimes called 'Ronsons', after the cigarette lighter that was supposed to 'light first time'. And the British Shermans were sometimes described as 'Tommy Cookers'. Once a Sherman had been hit, even if it did not result in an instant explosion, it was standard

WAS THE SHERMAN THE RIGHT TANK?

The Sherman tank was designed in the full knowledge that it could not match the firepower, nor did it have armour plating comparable to the German panzers. Moreover, its reputation for 'brewing-up' when hit meant that crews were quick to get out if a shell hit them, even if the damage it did was not fatal. Most crews describe the sobering experience of seeing their first brewed-up Sherman in battle – blackened and abandoned. And no one wanted to risk being burned alive or horribly scarred for life. The heaviest German tank, the mighty Tiger, weighing in at 56 tons and equipped with the all-powerful 88 mm high velocity gun, could take out a Sherman tank at 4,000 yards – whereas the Sherman could not penetrate the Tiger's frontal armour even at close range. Furthermore, the lighter German Mk IV tank, which made up about half of the tanks in a Panzer Division, fired a shell with a velocity 20 per cent greater than that of the Sherman.

Many have criticised the Sherman, both during the war and since, for being the wrong tank for the Allies to have mass-produced. A British Labour MP, Richard Stokes, criticised the War Office in the House of Commons in July 1944 for sending soldiers into battle knowing the weakness of the Allied armour – but he was firmly told that such criticisms were not in the public interest and should not be openly aired.

Why did the Americans not mass produce a heavier tank, like the T-20 which was in development for nearly three years? Probably it was a combination of a belief in the need for speed against weight, and an awareness that the Sherman was the perfect tank to mass produce. The amount of steel and armaments needed to mass produce a heavy tank like the T-20 would have been almost impossible to source. The belief in the Sherman was a belief in numerical superiority, which was fine on the grand scale. But in individual contests, the numerical advantage counted for little or nothing, and the Sherman crews sometimes began to feel that they were expendable.

practice to abandon the tank immediately – no one wanted to hang around and risk burning to death in the cauldron that might follow.

Each Sherman became home for its crew, who often lived in their tank for days on end and frequently slept alongside it – or even under it when the ground was hard enough to prevent the tracks from sinking in at night. Tank crews became closely bonded units with men

Moment of death! This British-manned Sherman has just received a direct hit and could 'brew-up' any moment. Surviving crew members have seconds in which to make their escape.

who would live, eat and sleep together for weeks on end. Frequently, in the British tank units men would address each other by their Christian names and sometimes the tank commander was not even called 'Sir' – rare in the rest of the hierarchical and often rigid military structure. Usually one member of the crew would be allocated various domestic duties – like brewing-up tea in a little stove that regulations strictly forbade the use of within the tank, or spreading jam on bread and biscuits for the rest of the crew. Often this was the job of the loader or co-driver who, when not in action, frequently had time on their hands. Most men adapted to their surroundings and found nooks and crannies to store books or letters from home. Although no more than a machine, the Sherman soon became a friend to the crew who got to live in it.

An attempted Allied landing at the French port of Dieppe in August 1942 proved a disaster. There was an appalling casualty rate. After Dieppe, British and American planners working on the invasion of Europe, realised the need for armour to precede the infantry ashore and to clear the many waiting obstacles. Speed was to be of the essence, both in crossing the beach defences and then in building up a bridgehead. The Germans were now busy around the clock laying mines along the north French coast – some four million would be laid before D-Day. Half a million troops and conscript workers constructed hundreds of concrete pill boxes and miles of iron and steel anti-tank

A quiet interlude for this Sherman crew of the 13th/18th Hussars. Two write home whilst others grab some sleep – the Sherman was their mobile home.

devices. Each landing spot was covered by enfilading fire from well defended redoubts and bunkers. This massive coastal fortress was known as the Atlantic Wall and in January 1944, Hitler appointed one of his favourite generals, Field Marshall Erwin Rommel, to take over the completion of the defences and the preparations to repel a probable invasion. Rommel's energy and determination brought a new vigour to the construction of this mighty coastal defensive barrier.

As the initial plans were laid for the invasion of Europe along the Normandy beaches, there emerged a need to develop the right sort of specialised armour to lead the invasion force. In the spring of 1943, General Sir Percy Hobart was put in command of the British 79th Armoured Division. Hobart, aged 58, was deemed too old to command a unit in action overseas. But he was a rare breed in the army. He had a fertile mind, immense amounts of energy, was always questioning things around him and would never take 'no' for an answer. After a distinguished career in the First World War, he had transferred to tanks in the 1920s and had been one of those involved with the experimentation in armoured warfare that had briefly placed Britain at the forefront of tank development in the early 1930s. He had the full backing of Prime Minister Winston Churchill and was now asked to come up with ideas for the sort of armoured vehicles that would help the invasion forces to get ashore across the Atlantic Wall and to build up a bridgehead. The 79th Division became known as the

As Field Marshal Erwin Rommel worked hard to improve the defences along the Channel coastline, Major General Percy Hobart, commanding 79th Armoured Division, had the job of overcoming those same defences.

'Zoo' as it experimented with a series of weird armoured machines designed to penetrate the Atlantic Wall.

The first of these devices, which became collectively known as 'Hobart's funnies', were swimming tanks with floating skirts around them, designed to go into the beaches in the first wave. On these DD Tanks (Duplex Drive) a large canvas screen was erected above the tracks to give the tanks enough buoyancy to float. Steerable propellers were driven from the tank's engine giving a speed of about 5 mph. The intention with the DD tank was that after landing on the beach it would be fully operational straight away. But the tanks could only operate in relatively calm seas. Churchill was delighted with the swimming tanks when he saw them demonstrated and hundreds were constructed. The Admiralty, however, remained convinced that they would never be seaworthy.

One problem with a beach landing was building up arms and vehicles where there were no roads and where the ground was soft. Daring teams of reconnaissance divers had landed on the Normandy beaches at night early in 1944 and brought back soil samples. Some of these proved that in places the sand was too soft to support armoured vehicles. Hobart and his 'think tank' came up with a set of Bobbin tanks which carried a metal track above the turret, with a feeder mechanism to lay this firm track across soft sand. Another problem was clearing minefields under fire. Flail tanks were built with a rotor

The first of 'Hobart's funnies' – the swimming Sherman. Provided that the sea was calm, and that the distance travelled through water was not too far, they were successful.

which projected on a pair of arms at the front of the Sherman, known as a 'Crab'. These rotors were turned and as they spun, a set of whirling chains flailed the ground, detonating any mines in front of the advancing tank. At one point in the development of the flail tank the army asked for thousands of yards of heavy chain to be forged, prompting the response from the tiny chain-making industry that to meet the order the Royal Navy would have to sacrifice its future supply of anchor chain! Bulldozer tanks were constructed to push aside heavy obstacles like the sea wall. And flamethrower tanks were constructed to flush out the enemy from well defended strongholds. They could fire a jet of flame about 100 yards.

Plans for the invasion of fortress Europe were practised and refined in repeated exercises across the south of England. Detailed timetables and operating plans for each of the five invasion beaches were drawn up by the US, Canadian and British commanders. DD Tanks slowly practised their descent into calm inshore waters as doubtful naval officers looked on. At the Orford tank training area in Suffolk, replicas of the Atlantic Wall were constructed complete with minefields and tank defences. They were assaulted by Hobart's men from a variety of different directions and with an assortment of new devices to find the most successful tank adaptations. Waterproofing kits were tried out with sealants designed by the Bostik company. AVREs (Armoured Vehicles Royal Engineers) were developed from the British Churchill tanks to allow engineers to dismantle beach defences from the

The Crab – Flail Tank – made an important contribution to the successful landings in Normandy, by clearing a path through the German minefields.

protection of a tank. Other tanks were adapted to lay bridges. When it was found that the clay along the Wash in Lincolnshire was similar to that under one of the invasion beaches, several tank landings were attempted along this stretch of coast to simulate landing in Normandy. Hobart's energy and inventiveness turned the British into pioneers of specialised armour with these tank variants. The Americans came and watched the exercises but were largely sceptical. They decided only to adopt the swimming tanks and not to take on any of the other specialised armour as part of their invasion force.

After months of planning, the invasion finally came at dawn on 6 June 1944. Dozens of tank landing craft, or LCTs, each carrying four of the American swimming tanks approached the US beaches code named Utah and Omaha. The swimming tanks were to be launched first to hit the beaches at H-Hour minus five minutes to help clear the defences for the infantry. But many of them were launched too far out and the seas were too rough. Tank after tank sank to the bottom of the sea – twenty-nine Shermans out of thirty-two in one group sank. Others were blown off course by the offshore winds and the tides. Moving at only 5 mph those that did carry on were an easy target. At Omaha one group of LCTs took their tanks right onto the beach to land them. But heavy defensive fire soon put most of them out of action. Armoured support for the first wave of the invasion had not been a

Sherman tanks of the 13th/18th Hussars aboard LCTs and heading for Normandy.

TI47161

success on the American beaches.

For the British and Canadian beaches, ten regiments had been trained by Hobart in the use of swimming tanks. At the eastern end of the invasion area, on Sword Beach, the landing drill worked perfectly. The sea here was fairly calm and most of the DD Tanks beached successfully. They covered the landings of the assault troops as planned and the Crab tanks flailed their way ashore clearing lanes through the mines. On the Canadian Juno Beach, the landings went more slowly and clearing obstacles proved difficult. But by late morning the bulldozer tanks went to work to clear the sea walls. Further west on Gold Beach the resistance was heavy in places and the sea was so rough that the DD Tanks had to be brought by the LCTs much closer in to the shore. Once on the beach the slow moving tanks proved horribly vulnerable to well placed German 88 mm and 105 mm guns. But the Crab Shermans flailed through most of the minefields and the Bobbin tanks laid carpets over the soft clay so the assault teams were at last able to knock out the German strongholds. By the end of the day, the British had lost thirty-two assault tanks out of 170 that had landed. The 79th Armoured Division lost a total of 179 men killed or wounded. These figures were dramatically below expectations. Armour had successfully been used for the first time to clear the beaches to enable the infantry to attain many of their first day

Shermans which failed to make it off the beach at Hermanville during the initial landings. The damaged floatation skirting can be clearly seen.

objectives. That evening Churchill paid special tribute to the 'ingenious modifications' of the British armour in a speech to a packed House of Commons. Hobart's funnies had more than proved themselves in their first day in action.

Despite heavy fighting and the loss of 3,000 Americans on Omaha Beach, D-Day had proved to be a great triumph. 177,000 men and their equipment were ashore. They had breached Hitler's supposedly impregnable Atlantic Wall. A bridgehead was quickly established. More armoured divisions came ashore in the days following. But once the Germans had properly recovered, a fierce battle ensued known as the 'Battle of the Hedgerows' after the characteristic feature of the Normandy countryside. These Hedgerows were well established banks of trees, hedges and undergrowth that lined almost every road and most of the fields in Normandy. They were ancient barriers, some of which dated back to the time of William the Conqueror. This was not good countryside for tanks to operate in. They were prevented from moving at speed by the narrow, bendy, often sunken roads; they could not see far over the high hedgerows, and the dense woods and orchards provided plenty of opportunities for ambushes. Armour would play a vital role on both sides in the battle for Normandy but it was now up to the infantry to fight their way out of the hedgerows.

Field Marshall Bernard Law Montgomery was commander of land

The narrow lanes and thick hedgerows of the Normandy countryside made advancing extremely difficult for the armour and provided good defensive positions for the Germans. A knocked out Kpfw IV is passed by a British manned Sherman.

forces in Normandy. Haunted by memories of the slaughter on the Western Front in the First World War, in which he had distinguished himself as a young officer, Montgomery was determined to avoid similar losses now he was in charge. Montgomery was also under political pressure from home. Britain's manpower was fully stretched and could not afford World War One type losses. Consequently, Monty's strategy was geared to advance with the minimum of loss. This gave Monty a reputation with the Americans for being over-cautious and he did not always see eye to eye with the Supreme Commander, General Dwight D. Eisenhower. But now Montgomery had a difficult task. He had to build up supplies and marshall his strength for a breakout from the bridgehead, whilst resisting fierce counterattacks by a determined enemy. Although the Germans failed to defeat the Allies on the beaches as Rommel had hoped, they committed more and more divisions to the Normandy campaign. Within a few weeks, two battle-hardened SS panzer divisions arrived from the Russian Front. By the end of June, about one million men faced each other across a front of approximately 100 miles in Normandy.

The Allied build up was immense. The Americans brought 81,000 vehicles ashore in the first 11 days after D-Day. Every GI required 30 lbs of supplies per day to keep him operating. British soldiers needed 20 lbs per day. All this equated to 26,000 tons of stores every single day.

An 88mm gun crew operating in the bocage during the 'Battle of the Hedgerows'. It was ideal country for the defenders and the Germans were able to set up many ambushes and employed tank-killer sections.

Newly landed men were astonished by the build up around them with giant dumps of fuel, ammunition and food, huge parks of new vehicles, tanks and artillery all lined up in neat rows. Everywhere there were field telephone cables and unit signposts directing men and materiel in every direction. Movement was often delayed by traffic jams and detours as the military police struggled to clear the congestion and to keep the armies moving. The main British Armoured Divisions started coming ashore from 7th June and found it increasingly difficult to find anywhere to assemble. Every field seemed to be taken. But still more and more men and machines were landed.

The build up continued until 18th June when unseasonal storms lashed the Normandy coast. Hundreds of ferries and landing craft were wrecked in the gales. The portable Mulberry harbours that had been brought over from England and positioned off the coast, were nearly destroyed along the American beaches. The amount the Allies could bring ashore dropped to 3,000 tons of supplies a day. This near catastrophe threatened to set back Montgomery's plans. But after a few days the storms blew over. The harbours and piers were mostly repaired and the vast supply machine went back into action once again.

Monty continued to maintain pressure on the Germans. The city of Caen, ten miles inland, had been an early objective of the D-Day landings but had been defended ferociously by the Germans, heavily reinforced by the 12th SS Panzer Grenadier Division composed largely

The build up of supplies and reinforcements pouring into the bridgehead in preparation for a break-out. These Shermans belong to the French 2nd Armoured Division.

of volunteers from the Hitler Youth and by one Panzer Division after another. The Germans tried repeatedly to split the beachhead and to drive the Allies back into the sea but as the smoke settled after each assault, the battle lines had changed very little. After a few weeks of fighting, the Normandy front began to appear a bit like the Western Front in the previous war. Neither side seemed to possess the strength to dislodge the other from well defended positions. Monty feared that he was being driven into a long, bitter war of attrition.

From 26th June, another assault to the west of the city of Caen, code named 'Epsom', with 60,000 men and 600 tanks, drew more and more German forces into the fight. Scottish troops in the 15th Division led the attack, described by the Germans as 'the furious Scotsmen'. They crossed the Odon River, advancing along a narrow front about 6 miles into the German lines in what became known as the 'Scottish Corridor'. At the end of June, the 9th and 10th SS Panzer Divisions arrived from the Russian Front having been transported by train across the whole of Europe. Before having the opportunity to regroup properly, they were thrown into a counter attack. Another division arrived from Belgium, the 1st SS Panzer Division 'Leibstandarte Adolf Hitler'. More armoured troops were sent by Rommel from St Lô to hold the line. Altogether the Germans assembled eight panzer divisions, six of which were SS units. Never before had so many SS men gathered in such a small area. The Argyll and Sutherland Highlanders, now out on a limb, held on tenaciously and the week long battle fought itself out in another stalemate.

The Allied infantry had suffered a mauling in 'Epsom' with nearly

THE 88mm GUN

The German 88 mm gun was a dual purpose weapon. It could be used as an anti-aircraft or an anti-tank gun. Its muzzle velocity was superior to anything in the Allied arsenal – a shell left its long barrel at 3,340 feet per second, against 2,050 fps for the Sherman's 75 mm gun. This, along with its considerable range, made it the most feared weapon by British and American soldiers in Normandy. When used against tanks it was a killer and a single round could destroy a Sherman or turn it into a ball of fire and smoke. Just the sound of it firing, a characteristic stoccato sound, could stop an advance in its tracks. Over and over again, a small number of 88 mm guns were able to halt an Allied advance. On the first day of Operation Goodwood, just four 88 mm guns took out 16 tanks and decimated C Squadron of the Fife and Forfar Yeomanry. Later that day, in the fog of battle, the same 88 mm guns opened fire in error on their own Tiger tanks. The shells penetrated right through the massive 100 mm armour plating. For one moment, the German Tiger crews feared that at last the Allies had produced a gun that could destroy a Tiger tank. Unfortunately, this was not the case. The 88 mm was probably the best gun produced by any nation during the Second World War.

one in four dead or wounded. But Montgomery's plan was for his British and Canadian forces in the Second Army to tie up as much German armour as possible around Caen, allowing the Americans of General Omar Bradley's First Army to make a clean breakout to the west. This strategy was working supremely well. The German armoured divisions were committed to responding to Allied actions and never had the opportunity to mount a major offensive of their own to throw the Allies back into the sea as Rommel had always planned.

The Americans fought their way slowly up the Cotentin peninsula and after two days of bitter house to house fighting captured Cherbourg, on 27th June. But now Monty ordered Bradley to begin his new assault 'with the greatest drive and energy' in the west. The First Army had grown in strength to fourteen divisions, against which the Germans could only muster six divisions. But the terrain favoured defence and Bradley knew that now heading south from the Cotentin peninsula, his attack against the wooded and well defended high ground of la Haye-du-Puits would not be easy. As the American assault to break out from the Cotentin began, von Runstedt the Commander in Chief of Army Group West requested permission to evacuate Caen. General Geyr von Schweppenburg, commander of Panzer Group West similarly requested to move his panzer units west from Caen. Hitler refused to give ground, as he had done at Stalingrad

General Geyr von Schweppenburg

SS Panzergrenadiers moving up to counter-attack during Operation Epsom, supported by Panthers. Never before had so many SS units been concentrated on one area.

and in North Africa, and responded by relieving both of his senior generals from their command. Rommel was told that 'the present lines are to be held' and was ordered to counter-attack wherever possible. The intense fighting in hedgerow country continued.

On the Allied side, Monty too was coming under increasing pressure to break through, and so now planned his biggest assault yet. This came to the east of Caen from July 18th and was code named 'Goodwood'. Wanting to avoid heavy infantry casualties like those he had endured in 'Epsom', Monty decided to use his armoured divisions for the thrust of the attack. Three armoured divisions would attack at Goodwood. Despite the arrival of the German panzer reinforcements, the Allies had built up a tremendous superiority in armour – the British tanks outnumbered the German panzers by four to one, the American tanks by eight to one. The plan for Goodwood was that three British armoured divisions would blast through an opening that had been made by heavy bombing of the German lines and reach highground to the south within hours. Then they would break out into open country and with Canadian support head south towards Falaise. Both Monty and Eisenhower had great hopes for the assault. Ike wrote 'I am confident that it will reap a harvest from all the sowing you have been doing during the past weeks... I am viewing the prospects with the most tremendous optimism and enthusiasm.' Monty needed a victory and this would be it.

Attempting to draw fire in the hedgerows – the majority of GIs had not been in action before and fighting conditions throughout the month of June were to prove a traumatic initiation to warfare.

At 5.30 on the morning of 18th July, more than 2,000 heavy and medium bombers of the RAF and the USAAF launched one of the heaviest ground support air raids of the war. Three waves of bombers hit the German defences causing immense damage. Guns were wrecked and twisted; defensive lines were shattered; tons of earth and rubble were showered down upon the defenders, some of whom were stunned for days to come. Most Allied observers believed that nothing could survive bombing on this scale and ferocity. Even the huge Tiger tanks could not withstand the might of aerial bombardment. As the Shermans advanced they found groups of German tanks, including the Tigers, destroyed by heavy bombs. In places, sixty tons of steel had been thrown into the air as though it were a matchbox. The sight of these heavy giants upended or turned over astonished the Sherman crews as they began their advance.

As the morning mist lifted, the Shermans of 11th Armoured Division began to move forward at H-Hour, which was 8.30 am. The tank crews of the 2nd Fife and Forfar Yeomanry leading the advance knew that this was what they had trained for and felt that nothing could stand in their way. The advanced squadrons of British Shermans crossed the River Orne over the bridges that had been captured by British paratroopers on the night before D-Day more than six weeks before. Five additional bridges had been constructed north of Caen. Crossing the river was slow and in the summer heat, the noise and the immense amount of dust thrown up by the advancing tanks gave away any possibility of surprise. One German divisional commander, Sepp Dietrich, used a primitive system to predict the advance of

THE PANZER MkVI – TIGER

The Tiger, weighed 56 tons, carried 100 mm of frontal armour and 80 mm of side armour and was almost impenetrable to any weapon possessed by the Allies. Its gun, a variant of the famous 88mm anti-tank weapon, could penetrate 120 mm of armour at 100 yards and could knock out a Sherman at 4,000 yards.

The specification for the Tiger prototype had been proposed by Hitler himself in 1941 and the first Tigers came off the production line in late 1942. They fought on the Russian front through 1943 in some of the greatest tank battles of the war. Tiger battalions were organised as separate units and were rarely used to lead attacks, which was left to the faster moving Panzer IVs. By 1944, several SS Panzer Divisions had been equipped with Tiger tanks but they were always few in number and in a minority.

The failings of the Tiger were in its slowness of movement and its lack of mechanical reliability. This meant that in the battle for Normandy the Tiger usually played a defensive role. Well dug in and camouflaged, it could hold up a Squadron of Allied tanks, or more. This suited the German position in Normandy which was primarily defensive – the Tiger would have been far less effective as an assault weapon, which the Sherman was designed to be. This fault, however, was not very apparent to those who came face to face with the most feared tank in the German arsenal.

opposing armour he had learned on the Russian front – he simply put his ear to the ground and could hear the distant rumble of the massed Allied armour as it approached. The supporting tanks took some time to funnel across the Orne bridges to follow up the attack. But for a few hours the leading Shermans advanced rapidly and forward units penetrated three or four miles. All seemed to be going well.

But by late morning, the Germans were beginning to recover from the shock of the aerial bombardment. Isolated units survived almost unscathed. One group of four Luftwaffe 88 mm anti-aircraft guns near the village of Cagny were intact. Panzer Colonel Hans von Luck instructed their commander to make the weapons over to anti-tank guns. The Luftwaffe 88 mm gun commander refused. Von Luck drew his pistol and threatened to shoot the gunner there and then unless he obeyed. The 88 mm commander agreed and opened fire on the advancing British Shermans. C Squadron of the 2nd Fife and Forfar lost sixteen tanks to these guns alone. The advance came to a halt. But the British units re-formed and continued the advance until the tanks came up against well hidden German panzers that had survived the air raids. Eight Tiger tanks formed up in a defensive line near the village of Manneville. With heavier and bigger guns than the Shermans they began to counter-attack during the afternoon.

The Sherman had been designed and built in the knowledge that its firepower and armour was inferior to that of the heavy German panzers. Now the reality of this came home. Over and over again in the battles around Caen, one German panzer was able to knock out four or five Shermans before being taken out itself. Now in the

Goodwood advance, several squadrons of British Shermans were surrounded by German panzers. By the end of the day, the 11th Armoured division had lost 126 tanks – half the division's strength. The Guards Armoured Division trying to cover the flank of the attack had lost sixty tanks. With this scale of losses the momentum of the British advance stalled.

That night the Germans reinforced the high ground of the Bourgébus Ridge with panzers from four divisions that were thrown into the defence. Next day they managed to hold on despite Canadian pressure driving out of Caen, finally clearing the eastern suburbs of the city. Over the next couple of days, the British Shermans hit back tenaciously at the German armour and by sheer force of numbers they captured most of the high ground that had been their objective. But the summer sun that had created a blanket of dust across the Normandy countryside was now replaced with torrential rain that turned the battlefield into a sea of mud. Against fierce and determined German resistance, Monty's massed tank assault slowed down and came to a halt. By 21st July Operation Goodwood was over. British tank losses amounted to 400 tanks – a third of their armoured strength in Normandy. The German line held. But Monty's plan worked in that more and more German armour was sucked into the battle in the east around Caen. At last, the moment for the big breakout to the west had come.

A section of German 'Tank Destroyers' (Panzerjäger) *moves through a Normandy village. The last man is carring a* **Panzerfaust***, a one-shot projectile effective up to thirty metres. Also he has two rockets for the* **Panzerschreck** *being carried by the third man.*

Throughout July, the American First Army under General Bradley had been bogged down along the front around St Lô. After 12 days of continuous fighting, VIII Corps had advanced seven miles but had suffered 10,000 casualties. More alarming to some observers was the high level of battle fatigue amongst the American soldiers – which accounted for almost 20% of all casualties. Whole units had to be withdrawn or were decimated by battle fatigue as the stiff German resistance and the difficulty of the terrain prevented a significant breakout. But gradually, the build up of men and machines became overpowering. On 18th July, the 29th Division reached positions overlooking St Lô, despite suffering more than 3,000 casualties. Along with the 35th Division they fought for the remains of the city which had been almost flattened by Allied bombardment and forced a German Parachute Corps finally to withdraw from the rubble, all that was left of the town.

On 25th July, after the rain finally ceased and the skies cleared, another huge Allied air bombardment launched the new American offensive designed finally to break out from Normandy, Operation Cobra. 2,000 Allied planes blasted the German defences behind the road running between St Lô and Periers. The American front-line units had withdrawn 1200 yards to give the Allied planes a safety margin for their bombing. The Americans watched the bombing from their foxholes and tank turrets. 'How gorgeous,' thought one young officer

This Canadian operated Sherman has received two hits, one on the hull and one on the turret, from a distance of 40 metres. Both have pentrated the armour.

as he watched the bombs destroy the German defences. But then the bombs started to come nearer and nearer and, as smoke filled the battlefield, in several places the Allied planes began to bomb American soldiers. 'Goddamit they're coming for us...' thought the same officer who had looked on with joy only a few moments before. Another soldier remembers how 'the ground was shaken and rocked as if by a great earthquake.' Over one hundred American soldiers were killed and nearly five hundred were wounded by their own bombs. This was the second successive day in which they had suffered from 'friendly fire' by their own aircraft. Local commanders were outraged and vehemently cursed the airmen.

The attack still went ahead later that morning across a four mile front led by VII Corps commanded by General J. Lawton 'Lightning Joe' Collins. But somehow the Germans managed to rally their dazed troops and the advance was slowed by a few stubborn defenders. Once again, a small number of 88 mm guns and a few heavy tanks prevented the Americans from breaking through as they had hoped on this first day. But although groups of Germans were resisting fiercely, they could no longer sustain a continuous line of defence. American units were able to outflank and isolate pockets of resistance whilst driving forward elsewhere. In any case, the German units in the west were weary and lacked the backing of the panzer units in the east around Caen. The Allied strategy was at last proving successful. Fourteen German divisions were tied up with the British and Canadians opposite Caen. But only eleven weakened divisions confronted the fifteen American divisions to the west of St Lô. One

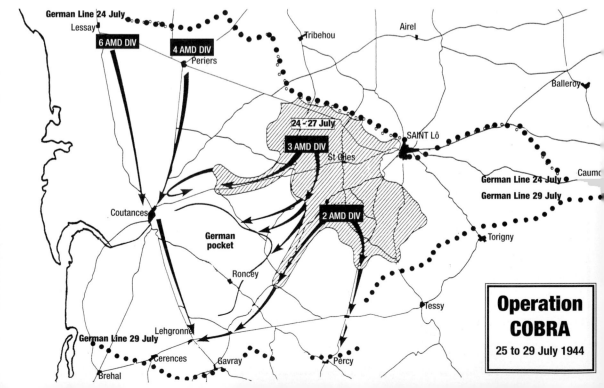

exhausted German officer, when told that under no circumstances was he to withdraw reported 'Not a single man is leaving his post. They are lying silent in their foxholes for they are all dead.'

On the evening of the 25th, 'Lightning Joe' Collins ordered his Shermans into action. By the next morning, the armoured columns were able to bypass the pockets of resistance and to move rapidly across country. The Sherman advance was now aided by a local invention called a 'Rhino'. Steel tusks were welded on to the front of several Shermans, enabling the tanks to force their way through the dreaded hedgerows that had been the curse of the fighting in Normandy. Now that the Shermans could bulldoze their way through these ancient obstacles they could at last begin moving across the open countryside. And this gave them the vital advantage of mobility. With American tanks charging forwards behind their lines, the German defenders had no choice but to withdraw. During the 26th July, when VIII Corps joined the Cobra assault further west, the German line began to crumble. The advanced columns of Sherman tanks were moving at speed, but behind them the infantry had to mop up the German line and round-up what rapidly became huge numbers of German prisoners who had decided the battle had been lost.

Within a couple of days the American advance was building up a real momentum. The Shermans raced through village after village and were given joyous receptions from inhabitants who were delighted to have been libereated so quickly and so whose homes and livestock had been saved from weeks of fighting. Allied aircraft and artillery would hit hard at any defensive groupings, a few tanks dug in here or a

GENERAL PATTON AND OPERATION FORTITUDE

Known as 'Old Blood and Guts', Patton had a ferocious reputation for taking the offensive – earned in the campaigns in North Africa and Sicily. Once an Olympic pentathlete, he cut a dashing figure in the smart cavalry uniform he still wore, glistening with his General's three stars on his helmet and his collar. He had been removed from command for slapping a soldier suffering from battle fatigue in Sicily and since then he had commanded only a pretend army gathered in Kent. This make-believe army, part of the plan code-named 'Operation Fortitude', consisted of plywood cut-outs, inflatable rubber tanks and other dummy vehicles and succeeded in deceiving the Germans that a major force was gathering in south-east England to cross the Channel at Calais. With Patton very publicly in command of this army, the Allies were superbly successful in maintaining the fiction that the Normandy landings were only a deception and the main invasion was still to come along the Pas de Calais. But watching events unfold in Normandy with no command role to play, Patton had been growing impatient. 'Time drags terribly,' he bemoaned to his wife, worried that the war would be over before he could make his mark again. Now Bradley, who had been Patton's deputy in North Africa and Sicily, recalled his former boss as commander of Third Army. Patton's moment had come.

couple of 88 mm guns there. The infantry, hitching a ride on the Shermans or marching through behind the tanks would consolidate the advance. A sense of exhilaration was spreading through the American camp. 'This thing has busted wide open' exclaimed one excited American commander.

On the 28th, Coutances, a vital strategic objective was captured. And on the following day, a considerable force of German tanks, vehicles and guns trying to escape was surrounded to the east of Coutances and pounded to pieces by American artillery and aircraft. German soldiers repeatedly found themselves isolated or cut off behind the American advance. Stragglers, or those dazed by the speed of the battle, were soon rounded up and taken prisoner. Others tried to press back to their own lines. Although there were fierce counter-attacks, often by groups of Panzergrenadiers who could be lethal in attacking the weakly armoured Shermans, the Americans began to realise that they were now dominating the battlefield.

During the last two days of July, the German defences collapsed along the coast. On 31st, both Granville and Avranches were captured. Armoured columns raced ahead and reached the River Sélune at Pontauban. To their amazement, the Sherman crews discovered that a crucial bridge over the river here had not been destroyed. It was seized immediately and provided a gateway into Brittany. Meanwhile, in the east, the Germans were holding firm and were clearly trying to wheel back their line, pivoting around the town of Vire to protect the line to the heavier defensive units that were still facing the British and

With bombs, rockets and cannon fire, the Allied air forces pounded German positions, armour and lines of supply. Such was Allied air supremacy that the Germans could only move safely at night. A Typhoon of the Royal Air Force is loaded with bombs during the Normandy campaign.

Canadians south of Caen.

On 1st August, a new US army group, the Third Army came into being to take command of VIII Corps and the advance into Brittany. Bradley brought back as commander of Third Army an old warrior who so far had not been allowed to participate in the battle for France, General George S. Patton. But Patton's new mission ideally suited his character, to clean up in Brittany and to capture the major ports – in short, to break out in the west.

The German army in Normandy was now reduced to only a fraction of its former strength. Nearly every active division had been decimated by weeks of intense fighting. Harried by constant attacks from the air, delayed by the plots of the Resistance in its rear, constantly suffering from a lack of petrol and ammunition, it is a fine tribute to the German fighting machine that it still managed to harass the Allies at every thrust they made. The fanatics of the SS fighting divisions defended their line furiously but for many soldiers, the will to fight on was slowly crumbling. Field Marshall Rommel had come to realise the fundamental weakness of the German position up against the might of the industrial democracies led by the United States. Very few tanks lost by the Panzer divisions were replaced. Almost every tank lost by the Allies was replaced within hours by the flood of new machines rolling off the production lines in Detroit. The losses in manpower by the Germans were final. The Americans appeared to

During Operation Cobra, a Sherman makes its way between two German MkIVs which have been knocked-out – probably by air attack judging by the condition of the smashed panzer in the foreground. Its mangled turret lies a good distance away, behind the camera.

have an endless supply of fresh, new divisions to bring into the fighting line.

Rommel began to believe that Germany's real interest lay in stopping the Russians from advancing across Germany and he started to toy with the idea of making peace with the Anglo-Americans in the west. After discussing this in a cautious way with some of his senior commanders on 16th July, he climbed back into his grand Horch staff car and sped back towards his headquarters. Just outside Vimountiers on the N179, an RAF Typhoon spotted the German staff car and opened fire. The car sped off the road and crashed into a tree. Rommel's driver was wounded and the Field Marshall was severely injured in the head. It was the end of Rommel's illustrious career as a battlefield commander. His successor as Commander of Army Group B was Field Marshall Gunther Hans von Kluge.

Ironically, when news of the 20th July Bomb Plot against Hitler reached the front, it probably helped to stiffen resistance. The attempt to kill the Fuehrer, on whom the adoration of the German nation had been focused for more than a decade, was thought to be profoundly un-German. The officers who had plotted were looked on by many fighting men as traitors. News of the Plot created immense tension between the diehard loyalists of the SS and the officers of the Wehrmacht who were thought to be trying to sabotage the German war effort. But despite the overwhelming odds stacking up against him, the German soldier continued to fight and to obey orders.

American infantry on the march as the German defensive lines crumble. The wrecked German MkV (Panther) receives the 'once over' from the GIs who could only note its obvious superiority to their own Sherman.

Within days of taking command of Third Army, Patton's Shermans were taking full advantage of the captured bridge at Pontauban over the Sélune river. Instructing his troops to flood across the bridge with maximum speed, two infantry and two armoured divisions crossed the bridge in 24 hours. Once across, Patton's divisions fanned out at the other side and raced into Brittany. In four days the Shermans of the 4th Armored Division advanced fifty miles to the town of Rennes. The Germans had never planned a major defence of Brittany and the surviving units there withdrew to the port towns to sit it out. Bradley's plan was to leave them 'to whither on the vine' and to keep up the momentum of the advance. Some German units survived intact until the end of the war in their isolated port fortresses. Elsewhere, the Wehrmacht was routed by the speed of the American Sherman advance. The German commander, Field Marshall von Kluge reported 'It's a madhouse here... Someone has to tell the Fuehrer that if the Americans get through... they will be out of the woods.'

One consequence of the Bomb Plot was that Hitler now lost all trust in his army commanders, from whose ranks the plotters had come. He therefore began to intervene more directly in matters of field command. Hitler sent a senior staff officer to von Kluge's headquarters to ensure that his orders were followed to the letter. Hitler's direct instructions were absolutely clear: 'You tell Field Marshall von Kluge to keep on looking to his front, to keep his eyes on the enemy and not to look over his shoulder.' Viewing the situation from his command headquarters in east Prussia, hundreds of miles from the front, Hitler decided to launch a counter-attack in the area of Mortain, hoping to

Surveying the situation in early August, von Kluge reported to Hitler:

'*Whether the enemy can still be stopped at this point is questionable. The enemy air superiority is terrific and smothers almost every one of our movements...Losses in men and equipment are extraordinary. The morale of our troops has suffered very heavily under constant murderous enemy fire...In the rear areas of the front, terrorists feeling the end approaching, grow steadily bolder. This fact and the loss of numerous signal installations makes an orderly command extremely difficult.*'

cut off the advancing American armies and to reach the sea at Avranches. His objective was to divide the Allied armies in half and force them back into the sea. With insufficient petrol and ammunition and given the strength of the American position, the plan was pure fantasy. But no one would dare to tell Hitler this.

Von Kluge was unhappy about transferring his armour from the Caen vicinity further west where he was potentially isolating them in an Allied encirclement. But in the wake of the Bomb Plot, von Kluge had to display super obedience or risk dishonour and possible arrest. Hitler's orders were clear. 'We must strike like lightning,' he commanded. 'When we reach the sea the American spearheads will be cut off. Obviously they are trying all out for a major decision here, because otherwise they wouldn't have sent in their best general, Patton...' Reluctantly, von Kluge ordered the remains of four panzer divisions to move west. There was endless discussion about exactly when the counter-attack should begin and von Kluge had minimal time for preparation. But after several phone conversations with Hitler during 6th August, the counter-attack was launched at midnight that night. It was named Operation Lüttich (Liège) after the town in Belgium from where Luddendorff had launched the dramatic assault on France, thirty years to the day before, in August 1914.

The attack began without any preliminary bombardment – partly because German artillery supplies were running low but chiefly to

Hitler with some well-wishers following the Generals' Plot to assassinate him. The explosion has left him with a trembling right-hand and he greets these fawning gauleiters with his left hand. Now that he distrusted his generals he interfered more and more in the running of operations in France.

create maximum suprise. British code-breakers at Bletchley Park had decrypted messages about the redeployment of the panzer divisions twenty-four hours in advance. But the midnight assault still caught the American ground troops around Mortain by surprise and to begin with made reasonable progress. However, as the morning mist lifted, the Germans dug in and covered their tanks with camouflage nets. 'Bad weather is what we need,' commented one German officer. But as the day cleared, the Allied air forces were able to strike at the armoured columns now stretched out clearly along miles of open road. RAF Typhoons and American Thunderbolts rained a deadly fire down on the panzers. The 2nd Panzer Division lost thirty of its remaining sixty panzers from air attack. For two more days there was fierce fighting. Isolated American units held on determinedly and in a range of heroic encounters fought off German assaults, mostly at night. The American line held until reinforcements arrived. Alerted by the Ultra decrypts, the 2nd Armored Division was on the scene within a couple of days. By then Operation Lüttich was effectively over.

From his faraway headquarters, Hitler fumed and talked of a second counter-attack and planned for more divisions to be sent to Mortain. But a new crisis was overwhelming the German army in Normandy and by 11th August the renewed attack was abandoned. The German armour that had been moved westwards for Operation Luttich was now deeper inside the American encirclement than they

This SS Panzergranadier is having his leg wound bandaged by a Medic. Because of their reputation for ruthlessness, captured SS men did not always receive such consideration from their captors.

had been at Caen. A disaster was approaching and even Hitler realised that he had to order his mobile units to start withdrawing. Still dubious about the loyalty of his army commanders, Hitler's verdict on Operation Lüttich was simple: 'The attack failed because Kluge wanted it to fail.' Conspiracies abounded at the Führerhauptquartier.

Whilst the US 30th Division was fighting bravely for its survival at Mortain, the Sherman tanks of Patton's Third Army had turned eastwards towards the mighty river valleys of the Loire and the Seine. On 8th August Le Mans was liberated. XII Corps headed due east towards Orleans. XX Corps headed north east towards Chartres and the direction of Paris. The newspapers were full of pictures of victorious Yanks, their helmets slanted back, sitting atop Sherman tanks and surrounded by rejoicing French civilians. Patton was basking in the glory this brought him. But, in truth, the Third Army were lucky. They came into being just as the breakout was beginning. Their triumph, magnificent as it was, was only possible because of the weeks of intense fighting that had preceded it. But for now, everyone looked on with amazement as Patton pushed his armoured columns further and further across the French countryside.

At this point Eisenhower and Bradley hatched a new plan. The centre of gravity of the American advance was hurtling eastwards, but the core of German Army Group B, because of Hitler's futile plan to counter-attack, had moved westwards. By directing Patton now to

Patton's Third Army was on the move – sweeping eastwards through northern France. He was then ordered to swing north as part of a pincer movement to cut off the German forces in Normandy.

turn north, and the British and Canadians to drive south, the Allies would have what was left of the German army in Normandy surrounded. Ike spoke to Montgomery on the phone and the appropriate orders were sent out. Whilst the embers of Operation Lüttich were still glowing, the Canadians launched Operation Totalize from the point south of Caen that the Goodwood battle had reached in July. The Canadian Shermans formed a spearhead behind which the infantry advanced in armoured vehicles. Again determined resistance by the 12th SS Panzer Division and a battalion of Tiger tanks, slowed the advance to a halt. A further thrust a few days later followed another gigantic air raid in which 800 RAF bombers dropped 4,000 tons of bombs. Now the Canadians finally achieved the breakthrough that was needed. By the evening of 14th August they were within sight of their objective – the ancient castle where William the Conqueror had been born at the town of Falaise.

About fifteen miles to the south, the advanced patrols of Patton's Third Army arrived at the town of Argentan. This was the new crisis that now befell von Kluge, who realised that the game was nearly up and his army was almost surrounded. Hitler agreed to what was officially termed a 'minor withdrawal' of his panzer units that were forty miles inside the Falaise pocket at Mortain. At last von Kluge could begin to prepare a defensive barrier. But his panzer units were desperately depleted. 1st SS had only thirty serviceable tanks; 2nd SS

A 'Tank-dozer' of 29th Infantry Division clears a way through the devastated streets of Lonlay-l'Abbaye.

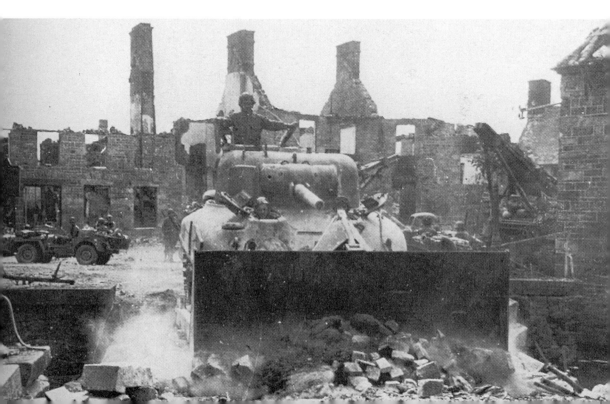

had only twenty-five; 116th Division only fifteen. Inside the Falaise pocket his men and surviving armour came under continuous attack from the air. Early on the morning of 15th August, von Kluge set off for a rendezvous with his deputy who was gathering the forces along his southern perimeter. An Allied plane spotted the Field Marshal's motorcade and attacked the vehicles. His radio car was destroyed and von Kluge had to take shelter in a ditch. Dodging fighter aircraft for hours on end, the Field Marshal never made the rendezvous and was incommunicado for most of the day. It was not until midnight that he was back in proper communication with the rest of his army – and with the Fuehrer.

Hitler described this day as 'the worst...of my life'. Waking to the news of the Allied invasion of southern France, Hitler knew that the French front was now impossible to defend. But he was even more worried by von Kluge's disapperance. Himmler had reported allegations that von Kluge was part of the Bomb Plot and Hitler imagined that von Kluge had given himself up to the Allies and was planning for the capitulation of Army Group B. By the time von Kluge was able to make contact again he had been replaced. Field Marshal Walter Model was sent to replace him, arriving on 17th August with orders now to carry out what von Kluge had long been hoping for, a complete evacuation of the Falaise pocket.

'If we can close the gap completely, we shall have put the enemy in

Shermans with supporting American infantry break out into open country.

the most awful predicament,' said Montgomery. And by now the German situation appeared hopeless. The remains of nineteen German divisions were caught inside a tightening noose. A German report summarised conditions inside the pocket: 'Roads virtually impassable, tanks repeatedly immobilised for lack of fuel, ammunition supplies erratic, troops hungry and exhausted, communications almost non-existent.' The only thing that allowed the Germans a few vital days (in fact nights, as movement by day was almost impossible because of constant harassment by air) to evacuate as many men as possible was Allied bickering. Bradley and Montgomery now failed in spectacular fashion to communicate and agree a plan to close the net around the Germans. They left a gap open between Argentan and Falaise and through this gap the Germans flooded from the night of 16th August. Despite continuous artillery and aerial bombardment the Germans managed to get some troops out. Many panzers and mechanised weapons were abandoned because of the lack of fuel.

Over the next few days the British, Polish and American troops closed the circle around the Falaise gap. Between 20 and 40,000 Germans got away by night. But when they closed the gap finally on 21st August, the scene inside the Falaise pocket was one of terrible carnage. The roads and fields were littered with German dead. There were smashed artillery pieces, trucks, wagons, and carts everywhere. Allied soldiers were amazed that as far as the eye could see there were

US Thunderbolt pilots are taken to view their handiwork – a type A Panther showing no obvious signs of damage.

dead horses and cattle swelling in the summer heat alongside the men and the wreckage of seven German Corps. 10,000 Germans were counted dead. 50,000 were taken prisoner. Like the British army at Dunkirk, the Germans had abandoned almost all their heavy equipment which had not already been destroyed. Von Kluge, now dismissed from his command managed to escape from the pocket and en route to Germany, knowing that the Fuehrer would blame him for the disaster, wrote a letter to Hitler saying that the war was as good as lost. Then he committed suicide with a potassium cyanide pill.

But the story of the Normandy breakout did not end there. With American tanks advancing at speed across France, the German army faced a complete rout. Four days after the Falaise gap was closed, on 25th August the German garrison in Paris surrendered. The Germans had plans to blow up Notre Dame and to block the Seine by demolishing the Eiffel Tower across it. Courageously, the commander there, von Cholitz, ignored Hitler's order to leave the city 'a field of ruins' and quietly departed. Gallantly, the Americans paused and allowed Free French soldiers to liberate their capital city. They raced 120 miles across France to be there. Fittingly, the 2nd French Armoured Division entered the city on Sherman tanks built in Detroit and supplied to them by the great Arsenal of Democracy. As the Parisian crowds came out into the streets mad with joy after years of brutal occupation, the first Allied war machines they saw were, of course,

On 21st August, the Allied encircling movement was completed and the German forces were trapped in the Falaise pocket. Roads leading eastwards to the River Seine were choked with smashed equipment. A Sherman rolls past two knocked-out Kpfw IVs

Sherman tanks.

The victory parade in Paris marked a truly immense triumph. Of the fifty infantry and twelve panzer divisions that had been thrown against the Allies in the weeks following D-Day, less than half were now able to line up in battle. In the Battle of Normandy, 2200 German panzers had been destroyed. Twenty-seven infantry divisions had ceased to exist. The victory in Normandy was on a massive scale, to be compared with Stalingrad or other gigantic victories on the Eastern Front. Despite Hitler's attempt to rally his Army Group West along the Somme and the Marne, the rout was too great. Everywhere, the surviving German units were heading east at full speed. It seemed to some observers that the way was now open for an assault against Germany itself.

At the forefront of the breakout and the advance that had crushed the German army in the west was one machine, the M4 Sherman tank. Stifled at first by the hedgerows of Normandy and always at a disadvantage when it came up against the superior firepower of the heavy panzers, especially the Tiger tank, it had finally showed what it was made for – mobile, aggressive, forward moving assault action. It was reliable and tough and was available in numbers that ultimately overwhelmed the battlefield. Driven by American, British, Canadian, French and Polish crews who were brave, committed and grew to respect their vehicles, the Sherman tank was ubiquitous in battle and was at the spearhead of victory in Normandy.

Carnage – German vehicles and casualties within the Falaise Pocket.

Free French tanks liberate Paris – a symbol of victory in the Battle of Normandy.

Chapter Six

'DUCK' LANDING

'It is important that the feet and clothes of the men landed should be kept as dry as possible if this can be done without prejudicing the speed of disembarkation; gang planks should always be provided, and they must be broad and firm'.

INSTRUCTIONS FOR DISEMBARKING TROOPS, ROYAL NAVY MANUAL 1939

Of all the machines created during the Second World War few can rival the DUKW for sheer originality. It was the truck that went to sea – an improbable but highly effective solution to an age-old problem. Its official name was the DUKW amphibious vehicle, but all who knew and operated the machine called it the 'Duck', and this account of its exploits follows their example. It was invented to act as a bridge between water and dry land and is still fondly remembered by the thousands who were spared a 'ducking' thanks to the Duck.

It is a tradition with soldiers that they do not like to get their feet wet. It makes marching a miserable, squelching ordeal and can

A determined-looking bunch of GIs pose for a publicity shot of the new amphibious contraption – the DUK or 'Duck', as it was affectionately named.

seriously reduce a unit's fighting ability. Water has always been the soldier's enemy and one of the most effective barriers against attack; the castle moat could be as daunting as its walls. Without a bridge, even a small stream can hold up an army on the move, crossing a river is a major problem. Bridges become key objectives to capture, or to hold, or to destroy.

From a soldier's point of view, the sea is definitely best left to sailors, unless you are that special breed of sea-going soldier – a Marine. But the need for co-operation is obvious: to cross the sea, an army needs ships, which are operated by navies, with their own ideas and traditions when it comes to fighting.

Combined Operations which involve more than one service, are an essential part of warfare but are fraught with problems of responsibility. Underlying any co-operative military venture are the two questions 'who gets the credit if it goes right?' and 'who carries the can if it goes wrong?' The dividing lines are often badly defined. In the 1930s, the British Navy informed its sailors that

> *'During the first phase of an opposed landing the Navy will be charged with the whole conduct of the arrangements for getting troops, guns and warlike stores disembarked, and will continue to be responsible for this part of the operation, at any rate until the landing is secured'.*

But who decides when the landing is secure? Conflicting views of the military situation, inter-service rivalry and personality clashes can

Overcoming a water obstacle during Wellington's campaign in the Peninsula. British troops crossing the Tagus, July 1811.

easily lead to friction. Too often, wind and tide also refuse to co-operate and things can go seriously wrong very quickly.

William Duke of Normandy – William the Conqueror – managed to pull off a successful invasion of England in 1066. His fleet of 700 boats carried some 11,000 soldiers across the English Channel, but the weather was good, he landed unopposed and did not have to fight the Battle of Hastings on the beach. The Spanish Armada, with fewer ships but twice the number of men, failed comprehensively in 1588. They were beaten, partly by the English Navy, but mainly by bad organisation, bad weather and bad luck. There have been successful amphibious raids throughout history, but the decisive battles have traditionally been fought on dry land – like Waterloo, or at sea – like Trafalgar, but not both.

As Europe fought its way through centuries of bloody conflict, the amphibious attack was always feared and always expected. The Southern coast of England is still dotted with elaborate coastal defences, designed to protect vital harbours like Portsmouth from a seaborne attack. But the logistical problems of getting an entire army onto a fleet of sailing ships, crossing the open sea and disembarking on a hostile shore were so daunting that it was rarely attempted.

Even on dry land, an army on the move was an unwieldy operation, strung out for miles with very little communication between the head of the column and the lumbering supply train bringing up the rear. It was manned by a lowly rabble of assorted non-combatants – which

At the start of World War Two, the British strategy for mounting an amphibious operation had barely changed since the days of Nelson's Navy.

often included the wives and children of the fighting men.

By the time of Napoleon the Supply Train had grown into a huge operation – an army within an army. Officers would fill their tents with quantities of personal items like campaign chests, map tables, camp beds, chairs and dressing cases. The whole lot had to be transported by an ever-growing fleet of wagons. An army encampment began to resemble a frontier town, with rows of tents, field kitchens and an assortment of tradesmen like bakers, blacksmiths, leather workers and coopers, keeping the men fed and the equipment in working order.

Then came the First World War and the full horror of mechanised warfare was unleashed in a stream of high-explosive shells, mortar bombs, hand grenades and machine gun bullets – all of which had to be constantly replenished. As the war bogged down in the trenches of the Western Front, supply became the most important factor in the absurd deadlock. By hurling an equal tonnage of deadly projectiles at each other, the armies made sure that neither side could advance. Every single item needed to sustain the soldiers in the front line trenches, had to be brought in through the wasteland of churned up mud and debris and the fighting men spent long hours shifting it all, usually under cover of darkness. Drinking water and bully beef, duckboards and barbed wire, starshells and ammunition were all

Supply lorries loading up at a railhead on the Western Front during the Great War. The efficient and constant flow of supplies had become a major factor in the conflict.

carried up the narrow communication trenches from supply depots in the rear.

Behind the trenches, horses and mules still played a vital role in battlefield transport. In the first year of the war the British alone used more than 100,000 animals, but the loads quickly became too great for them to handle. New methods began to be used. Each side constructed networks of narrow-gauge railway lines through the blasted landscape. Every day they delivered huge tonnages from supply dumps in the rear to the battlefront. The dumps were supplied by the main line railway system and by a new invention, the motor lorry.

World War One was to change the whole concept of the battlefield. Mechanised battles were fought round the clock in impossible conditions: blinding snow, pouring rain, freezing cold and blazing heat. Battlefields were reduced to liquid mud, or swirling dust, but the killing went on unabated. By the end of the war, in 1918, battles had been fought in the sky and underwater, in baking deserts and frozen wastes, in mountain passes and in city centres. And they were fought on beaches.

The beach is a terrible battleground at the best of times. A narrow strip of soft sand when the tide is in, an open and exposed field of fire when it's out. Every body – and every thing – usually gets soaking wet: sand and salt water play havoc with weapons and machines. It's the location that nobody would chose for a fight and yet it's where many of the key battles of World War Two took place. In a land battle,

MOTOR TRANSPORT OF SUPPLIES

When World War One began in 1914, the motor industry was less than twenty years old, but primitive trucks were already capable of transporting several tons of cargo. They were slow and unreliable, their solid rubber tyres soon rutted the French roads and they were forever breaking springs or getting stuck in mud or potholes. But they steadily improved and by 1918, when the war ended, the British Army was operating a fleet of 33,500 trucks, as well as some 14,000 motor cars. The army truck was firmly established as an item of military equipment.

During the 1920s, improvements were made: drive shafts replaced chains, pneumatic tyres replaced solid rubber, engines became more powerful and more reliable. By the 1930s, the horse was being rapidly phased out of British and American military operations. Surprisingly, despite their advances in mechanised warfare, the Germans employed more than two million horses for supply work throughout World War Two, long after the Allies had relegated most of them to ceremonial duties only. In really bad conditions, the pack animal was still the only practical method of transporting supplies, but most transport in World War Two relied on millions of motor vehicles.

fought on level ground, two armies of equal size and equally well equipped, should stand an equal chance of victory. To mount a seaborne invasion, the attacker must have a vastly superior force of men and equipment, simply to equal the odds. To stand a good chance of winning, he probably needs to re-double his strength.

When America entered World War Two, in December 1941, the task ahead was daunting. Both Germany and Japan held large areas of land, which would have to be recaptured if they were to be beaten. In most cases, there was no land route available, they would have to be taken from the sea. Firstly, North Africa had to be invaded and cleared of Axis forces. In Europe; Sicily, Italy, southern and northern France would all require huge amphibious landings. In the Pacific; Japanese-held island chains, like the Philippines, the Marshalls and the Marianas, would have to be taken the same way. From Iwo Jima to Normandy, Allied soldiers would be forced to struggle ashore, under fire, on exposed beaches.

With the prospect of large-scale amphibious operations ahead, the Allied military planners tried to envisage, and solve, the massive problems that would arise. The first task would obviously be to put thousands of men ashore on open beaches as quickly as possible and the first question was how was it to be done without unacceptable losses? The British Navy manuals of 1939 had very little to offer. The approach was 100% traditional and seemed to be almost entirely lacking in imagination.

THE DARDANELLES

With World War One deadlocked in the trenches of the Western Front, Winston Churchill, then First Lord of the Admiralty, conceived a bold plan. He proposed to outflank Germany by sending a naval force into the Black Sea, to link up with the Russians, who were fighting Germany on the Eastern Front. But first, an amphibious landing would be needed to defeat Germany's ally Turkey, who held the narrow entrance channel to the Black Sea, known as the Dardanelles.

The plan was to attack the Turkish fortifications at Gallipoli. The combined assault force of British, Australian and New Zealand troops was more than 70,000 strong. Against them the Turks had only 15,000 men, but they held high ground and were well armed. The operation saw the first serious attempt to use a specialised landing ship. The collier 'River Clyde' was adapted, with exit doors cut in the sides and ramps for the troops to reach the shore. But the landing was a disaster from the word go and vividly demonstrated the perils of beach warfare. The ship grounded in water which was too deep for the troops to reach the shore. They had to be transferred into barges under heavy fire and suffered appalling casualties.

On other beaches, the situation was no better. Open boats and barges gave no cover for the troops and thousands were killed or wounded. Once ashore there was very little cover and even less hope of dislodging the Turks from their positions. After some nine months of clinging pointlessly to a few strips of bloodstained sand, the force was withdrawn. The Dardanelles was a humiliating failure, which stopped the mighty British Empire dead in its tracks. It eventually tied up half a million Allied troops and cost the lives of more than 25,000 of them, with 88,000 wounded. It convinced many senior military leaders that an amphibious assault against well defended positions was impossible.

'Best type of boats. – It will generally be necessary to use those of the existing naval type. Of these, naval cutters are the best for landing on an open beach. Transport lifeboats may also have to be used.

Horse Boats. – These form a convenient means of landing troops, animals and vehicles. They afford more protection from rifle and machine gun fire than an open boat. They are fitted with a hinged gangway in the stern and can be beached in 2.1/2 feet of water. When close inshore they should be towed stern first. When used for embarking or disembarking men carrying rifles and equipment, much time is saved if a substantial step in the nature of a wooden box about 3ft. x 2ft. x 1.1/2 ft is provided'.

The nightmare vision of un-powered boats intended for horses being towed backwards towards a beach, while under fire and of men then clambering out of them with the aid of improvised wooden boxes, seems almost farcical. Apart from the reference to rifles and machine guns, the above could have been the instructions for a naval landing in 1739, rather than 1939. There is no concept of a purpose-built landing craft, only thoughts on how unsuitable craft might be adapted. America too was surprisingly backward in the 1930s, also using conventional boats without bow ramps to land troops on beaches, thus forcing the soldiers to jump into water that could be waist-deep. Clearly the Allies had to have a proper landing craft before any effective amphibious operations could be seriously considered.

The landing craft was a fairly straightforward concept. Make an

HANDLING SUPPLIES

The weekly shopping trip to the supermarket is much like a military supply operation: it involves constant trans-shipping and depends almost entirely on wheeled transport. Every tin of beans in the shop is brought in by truck, off-loaded, ferried to the shelves by trolley and off-loaded again. The shopper transfers it to another trolley, unloads it at the checkout, reloads and wheels it to the car park, where it is transferred to the motor car, which carries it home, to be unloaded yet again and carried to the kitchen cupboard. Later the empty tin will be loaded into a truck for its final trip to the dump.

To function properly, a family needs a regular supply of everything from bread and milk to light bulbs and matches. A modern army has most of the same basic needs, but on a gigantic scale, involving thousands of tons of equipment and supplies, all of which have to be loaded, carried and unloaded. It all takes precious time and ties up large numbers of fighting men, as well as exposing them to increased risk of attack. It's a problem that has grown to dominate all aspects of military planning and anything that speeds up the labour-intensive business of supply is welcomed. Cutting out just one handling operation can save thousands of wasted man-hours.

oblong steel box, fit an engine, propeller and rudder at the back end and a hinged ramp at the front, and you have a practical system for delivering men and equipment onto a beach. It took an American, Andrew Jackson Higgens to make it happen. Working against much entrenched opposition in the U.S. military, he produced a simple but effective design which a least gave the soldier a fighting chance of reaching the beach.

Getting the men ashore would be only the first step. The military planners knew that any invasion would have to be backed-up by many thousands of tons of equipment. Weapons and ammunition, food and water, fuel and oil would be needed in huge quantities. Not to mention tents, blankets, field kitchens, mobile workshops, telephone cable, ropes, pierced steel planking and the thousand and one other things that an army depends on. Mechanised warfare is only efficient when it works. Having discarded the horse, the sword and the spear, an army can no longer forage for its supplies or live off the land. It needs ammunition of the right calibre and fuel of the right type. Even a weapon as powerful as a tank becomes impotent if it can't shoot or move. The mechanical warhorses quickly become more like beached whales, helpless without a reliable supply line and the army that depends on them soon grinds to a halt.

As a prelude to a full-scale invasion of mainland Europe, the Allies decided to mount a cross channel raid on the French port of Dieppe in August 1942. Despite having effective landing craft, the operation was a total failure, involving the loss of all 27 tanks that were put ashore and some 3,500 men. Putting a brave face on the disaster, Churchill described it as 'a reconnaissance in force'. Its only real value was to demonstrate the near impossibility of capturing a well defended port facility.

Assuming that any successful invasion would involve open beach landings, the ocean-going support ships bringing in supplies would be unable to reach the shore. They would have to anchor in deep water while their cargo was unloaded into a fleet of smaller vessels which could land on the beaches. At the water's edge, their cargo would have to be trans-shipped again into trucks and driven to the battlefield as it moved steadily inland. The process would be slow, labour-intensive and vulnerable to attack. On a falling tide, the boats could become stranded; on a rising tide, the trucks could be swamped if they got stuck in the sand. In addition to flat bottomed landing craft for putting the troops and heavy tanks ashore, some form of freight shuttle was needed, preferably some kind of modified landing craft which could actually climb out of the water and up the beach to safety before unloading. Better still would be a truck, able to swim between the ship and the shore, then drive up the beach and take to the road, delivering its cargo direct to the battlefield.

The floating truck sounded like a highly improbable machine under even the most favourable circumstances. Designing one that could drive through pounding surf and go out to sea seemed almost impossible. But it was achieved, creating one of the most unlikely vehicles ever seen on the road – or at sea: the DUKW, known to the G.I. as the 'Duck'.

The most obvious problem, and there were plenty more, was that any hybrid design would have to be a compromise. Trucks and boats are entirely different machines, operating in different mediums. The most likely outcome of any cross-breeding would be a device which was un-seaworthy when afloat and like a fish out of water on land. Since water is a much more hostile environment than land, it was logical to produce a boat-based design – a landing craft with wheels. But flexibility was going to be the key to the vehicle's success in operation and that pointed towards a truck-based solution.

What finally took shape was hardly inspiring to look at. The pilot's saying 'if it looks right, it'll fly right' certainly didn't apply to the Duck. It was slab-sided and ungainly, angular and badly proportioned, looking more like a builder's skip on wheels than a practical vehicle – but it was also inspired. The Duck remains one of

Part truck, part boat, the DUKW introduced a new and revolutionary type of military vehicle to the battlefield.

the truly great American wartime inventions: a bold and outstandingly successfully solution to an almost impossible problem. Once it had been invented, it seemed such an obvious idea – like the pop-up toaster or the non-stick frying pan, but to actually produce a truck that could go to sea, was a very tall order. Most good ideas are developments of earlier ones. Before the Duck could happen, there had to be a reliable chassis to base it on – fortunately for the U.S. Army, there was. It was known as the GMC 6x6, a two and a half ton truck, which first appeared in 1941.

The General Motors Company, or GMC, was formed in 1908 by the amalgamation of two of America's first truck builders. The American Army had used standard commercial trucks in the First World War. But they were not suited to battlefield conditions and a purpose-built army truck was clearly needed. In the 1920s and 30s, Americans were determined to keep out of European wars and the development of all military equipment, including motorised transport, was neglected by the Government.

In 1940, with all of Europe apparently about to fall under the control of Adolf Hitler's Germany, America belatedly embarked on a massive rearmament programme. GMC had a solid reputation as a builder of commercial vehicles, including the familiar yellow school bus, and were a natural choice when it came to finding a source of army trucks. It was proposed that a standardised range of trucks and utility vehicles

THE GMC 2.1/2 TON TRUCK

The 2.1/2 tonner was the ideal vehicle for the army and the most widely used version was the GMC, known to the American G.I.s as the 'Jimmy', or the 'Deuce-and-a-half'. It combined all the best qualities of reliability and versatility. It quickly became the most useful component of any transport fleet and was the ideal partner to the light-weight Jeep.

In the muddy conditions that quickly develop during military operations in wet weather, a wheeled vehicle without tracks, needs enough traction to pull itself out of trouble and enough wheels to spread the load. The GMC was known as a six-by-six, meaning that all its six sets of wheels were power driven. The wheels on the two rear axles were doubled up in pairs, giving a total of ten tyres to carry the load. In extreme cases, the front wheels could also be doubled up to make it twelve tyres. The off-road load capacity of 2.1/2 tons gave a gross weight of about seven tons and a load per tyre of well under a ton. On a hard road, the truck could increase its load to 4.1/2 tons. The GMC was tall and narrow, with a slightly top-heavy appearance, but was usually stable in service. Its high ground clearance of 17in avoided most debris on the road and coped well with rough conditions. It could ford water to a depth of 2ft 6in and climb a 65 degree slope in low gear. On a good road it could run at 50mph.

With a range of bodies fitted to its chassis, the GMC could become almost anything that the Army wanted it to be. It was a flat-bed or a tipper, a crane or a winch, a tanker or a rocket launcher. It could tow a trailer or a field gun. Specialised enclosed bodies included mobile workshops, radar stations, telephone exchanges, dental clinics and field dressing stations. With its road wheels replaced by flanged railway wheels, it could even be improvised as a locomotive, with a haulage capacity of about 100 tons on dry rails. All this versatility made it the obvious choice when the military began to consider the problem of the amphibious truck.

should be built, ranging in carrying capacity from half a ton to six tons. The most numerous type would be the two and a half tonner. By the end of the war in 1945, more than 800,000 had been built, 600,000 of them were GMCs. Their role extended far beyond the transport of supplies and their ability to carry men was often as important as their load hauling capacity.

Modern, articulated trucks can carry huge loads and the two and a half ton army truck of World War Two would be regarded as tiny by today's standards. But when working under battlefield conditions, large and heavy items, needing cranes and big vehicles, quickly become impossible to deal with. Cargo needs to be broken down into small units that can be easily handled by one or two men. With fleets of small trucks, large tonnages can be moved without the need for special handling equipment. Small trucks make less obvious and less inviting targets and limit the amount of cargo lost if a vehicle is destroyed. They can pass each other on narrow roads and can work on soft ground with less danger of becoming bogged-down. Although tracked vehicles cope far better with soft or uneven ground, they are usually slow and can be awkward to repair in the field if a track comes off.

European roads in the 1940s were mostly a legacy of the horse-drawn era. They were narrow and passed through towns and villages, rather than by-passing them. Many were still no more than compacted

stone, without a tarmac surface. Rail was still the normal method for transporting heavy loads. The U.S. Army had a large railway operating division within the Transportation Corps and based most of its strategy on the assumption that railways would be available, in Europe at least, for long-haul work. Trucks would be needed to distribute the loads from railheads, or to act as a stop-gap while damaged tracks were repaired.

When America entered the war, following the Japanese attack on Pearl Harbour in December 1941, a Government department was hurriedly set up to develop specialised military equipment. America would be fighting on at least two fronts: in the Pacific, with its chains of coral islands, and on mainland Europe. The North African desert was also likely to be an operational area. The brief of the Office for Scientific Research and Development (O.S.R.D.) was to find new ways of dealing with the problems likely to be encountered in the very different theatres of war. It was staffed by experienced engineers and managers, seconded from American industry.

One department specialised in transport problems. It was led by Hartley Rowe, the chief engineer of the United Fruit Company. His company was used to the problems of handling cargo over beaches in remote locations, without port facilities. To help tackle the amphibious truck project, he recruited a friend – Palmer Putnam – who was a keen yachtsman. Putnam recommended asking Rod Stephens to join the team. Stephens was well known as a designer and builder of racing yachts: in 1937, one of his designs had won the prestigious Americas Cup race. A floating truck seemed an unlikely project to interest a race

THE PIONEER SPIRIT

In the 1940s, the men who set out to create an amphibious truck, tackled the problem with the same spirit and the same open minds as the pioneers of the Old West. The American backwoodsman has always had a knack of finding the solution to a mechanical problem. He would often sink mine shafts, shift boulders, or haul the logs to build his cabin, with nothing more than ropes, wedges and levers. When Henry Ford's Model T car put America on wheels, the same spirit survived. The farmer would go to town in it, but he would also use it to pull his plough, or jack it up and drive a saw bench off its back axle. He was simply carrying on the very American tradition of inventive improvisation which was ready to forget convention and play a 'hunch'.

The West was opened up by the horse-drawn 'Prairie Schooner' – the covered wagon immortalised in the Hollywood Western. It was really just a simple farm cart, which could be adapted to a whole range of tasks. Its solid construction and high ground clearance coped with all but the most rugged terrain. If the going got too rough, the wheels could be taken off and, given enough manpower, it could even be picked up and carried. In snow it could be dragged like a sledge. When the trail crossed a river, the wagon became a boat and would be floated across. It was a home from home and could become part of a mobile fortification system. To 'circle the wagons' is an expression which still resonates today, evoking images of determination in the face of adversity.

It would take plenty of determination before the 'Duck' took to the water.

Rod Stephens

winner, a bit like asking a sprinter to design a pair of diving boots, but he responded enthusiastically. His first design was for an amphibious version of the Army's lightweight, four-wheel-drive, general purpose vehicle – the Jeep. Known as the 'Seep', it performed fairly well in water, but was found to be of very limited use as a load carrier.

Rod Stephens was then asked to adapt the GMC truck chassis, drawing on his development work with the Jeep. He was put in charge of a small team of civilian engineers and based at the GMC plant at Pontiac, Michigan. The Army viewed much of the experimental work done by O.S.R.D. with little enthusiasm and a good deal of suspicion. The soldier in the field has always tended to dismiss the 'new-fangled' inventions and stick to known methods. The reasoning is based partly on a resistance to change in any form, but mainly on the undeniable fact that the more complex an invention is, the more likely it is to go wrong. Under battlefield conditions, machines regularly break down, due to rough handling or a lack of proper maintenance, or both. As late as World War Two, even the highly mechanised German Army still depended on huge numbers of horses and carts, primitive but reliable relics of the past, in the age of the truck and the tank.

The amphibious truck seemed particularly hare-brained to some of the Generals and after reluctantly accepting the construction of four prototypes, the Army changed tack and proposed to cancel the whole project. Only after much persuasion did they agree to a single prototype. Work began in April 1942. Stephens and his small team of four specially selected GMC engineers set to work with a will. In only thirty-eight days, they produced the very first amphibian. It was given the standard GMC code letters D (1942) U (amphibian) K (front-wheel-drive) W (rear-wheel-drive). When the American G.I. eventually met up with the unpronounceable DUKW he soon gave it the phonetic name of 'Duck' which, being another ungainly amphibian, felt right. The name didn't sound exactly warlike and provided plenty of verbal ammunition for critics to throw at it: 'sitting', 'lame' and 'dead' were the most obvious. But its supporters could fight back with proverbs: it performed 'like a duck takes to water' and any criticism was 'water off a duck's back', etc.

The Duck was a standard GMC six-by-six truck chassis, encased in a steel hull. Its three axles, and their wheels, projected through the sides of its lower section. All possible points where water or sand could penetrate were sealed, with thick grease packed into all the vulnerable wheel bearings and steering joints. The power source was a hefty six-cylinder petrol engine of 4.5 litres, giving 91 horse power.

Like the GMC truck, the Duck could carry 2.1/2 tons of cargo or 25 troops. Protected in a tunnel under the rear of the hull, a propeller was mounted on a projecting shaft, driven off the gearbox. There was a conventional rudder at the rear and the two front wheels also acted as rudders at the front, all three being controlled by the steering wheel.

The hull was 31 ft long and slightly more than 8ft wide. It was decked in for about half its length leaving a rectangular space for the two crew seats and the cargo hold, surrounded by a raised rim to keep out water. Since shipping water would be a constant hazard, it was fitted with three separate pumping systems, giving a combined capacity of more than 300 gallons a minute, enough to cope with water flooding in through a three-inch shell hole for example. When working in rough sea, or beaching in heavy breakers, front and rear surf boards could be raised to deflect the water. In extreme conditions, an overall canvas cover could also be erected, effectively converting the Duck from an open to a closed truck and keeping out the worst of the spray. If it managed to get ashore safely, a series of drain plugs could be opened to release any water left in the hull. The important thing then was remembering to close them again, before re-entering the water!

It was put through a series of tests – in the water, first in the shelter of Chesapeake Bay, then in the Atlantic breakers – and on rough land. It came through with flying colours, performing surprisingly well in heavy surf. The Army remained typically unenthusiastic, but one

Training drivers to handle the new amphibious vehicle. The calm, off-shore waters of the United States were no preparation for the pounding surf they would face in the Pacific.

Colonel – A.C. McAuliffe – had been given the task of helping to plan the invasion of Europe. He was impressed by the Duck's performance and persuaded the Army to place an order with GMC for 2,000 Ducks. Production began but, as they left the factory, the Ducks went straight into storage and it became clear that the Army had no plans to repeat the order. It began to look as if the Duck would not get a chance to prove itself in action before a European invasion and would probably play only a minor role even then. Many of the military planners saw no need at all for such an unconventional machine and believed that it could prove to be a liability in combat.

Rod Stephens and his team became increasingly frustrated and concerned by the lack of official interest in the amphibian. They remained convinced that the Duck had enormous potential and finally persuaded the Army to agree to a major demonstration of its performance at Provincetown, near Boston. Realising that this was probably their last chance to convince the sceptics, they planned to put on a good show. But they could never have predicted the strange turn of events which would transform the 'ugly duckling' into something more like a swan, as far as the Government was concerned.

Four days before the demonstration was due to take place, a violent storm struck the area. A yacht belonging to the American Coastguard service was swept onto a sandbar a quarter of a mile off Cape Cod. Strong winds and heavy surf made it impossible to launch a rescue boat and the yacht was too far away from the shore to be reached by rockets and life-lines. After several failed rescue attempts, the local Coastguard Commander, who knew about the planned testing of the Ducks, contacted Stephens and Putnam and asked if they would risk taking one out to the wreck. They agreed and set off into the pounding surf. In less than ten minutes they were back, having successfully taken off the seven man crew of the stranded yacht. Only a few hours later, the wreck had vanished.

Two days later in Washington, the Secretary of War announced to a Cabinet meeting at the White House that an army truck had gone to sea and rescued the crew of a Coast Guard vessel. The laughter turned to gasps of admiration as he explained what had actually happened and how well the Duck had performed. Everybody, from President Franklin Roosevelt down to the officials responsible for the military budget, was suddenly interested in this exotic creature. Another (very well attended) demonstration was organised and most of the doubters were convinced. Here, it seemed, was the answer to the problem of ship-to-shore transport. One Admiral said 'this is like comparing an eight-cylinder Cadillac with a horse and buggy.'

Mass-production began in earnest and although some 800 small modifications were made during a production run of over 20,000, the basic design remained the same throughout the war. An early problem for the Military was trying to decide who should operate the Duck. Was it a boat, and therefore part of the Navy's responsibility, or was it still an army truck? The Navy was in no doubt about the matter: it floated, so it was obviously a boat. But huge numbers of landing craft were also beginning to be produced, and the Navy soon had to admit that it couldn't provide and train enough crews to operate all of them, let alone the amphibious trucks. They reluctantly accepted that the Army should operate the Ducks, on land and at sea.

The Army Transportation Corps was given the task of training the Duck crews, but soon found that it had a lot to learn from the Navy. Duck operation in water was far more than just a truck driving job. It involved an understanding of basic navigation, currents, wind speed, signalling and a whole range of seamanship skills that meant little to the average truck driver. Although the Duck could reach 50 mph on the road, its speed in water was only about 6mph. When caught in a strong current, or crossing a fast flowing river, it could become almost impossible to control. Realising the specialised nature of the task, the Army set up the Engineer Amphibian Command in the summer of 1942 and began an intensive programme of training, often based on improvisation and guess-work, since there was no existing Duck operator's manual to study. Their first task was to write one. Training took much longer than expected, partly because there were rarely enough machines available to practise on. It was eventually established as a five week course.

Although the Duck was a highly effective machine, it was far from perfect. It needed constant maintenance to remain serviceable. The deadly mixture of corrosive salt and abrasive sand, found its way into every crevice and for each hour spent in the water, twice as many had to be spent draining out, washing down and greasing up. Tyres and air pipes were often damaged by sharp rocks or underwater debris. The first operational Ducks were sent to the Pacific and reports of problems soon began to filter back. Mechanical faults began to show up, a legacy of its rushed design and construction. Most were not serious, but the number of Ducks out of service was often unacceptably high. More serious was the inability of the crews to handle their machines properly.

The Duck units soon found that training in calm water off the coast of Virginia, was no preparation for the breakers crashing on the coral reef of a Pacific island. Roughly one in every six crewmen had to be re-assigned as unsuitable for Duck operations. Training was made more realistic and more demanding, and the figure was gradually reduced to about one in twenty. The level of training that the crews had been given usually dictated the success of any military operation involving Ducks. The regular soldiers were often more willing than the Marines to accept the Duck's shortcomings in water and liked its ability to function as a truck on land. Unfortunately, the army drivers tended to instinctively head inland and avoid going to sea if possible, meaning there were rarely enough Ducks available for the vital ship-to-shore work.

Although it was one of the most versatile tools the military possessed, the Duck came in for more than its share of problems, most of which were not its fault. One very basic mistake often made during the early days of Duck operations, was the rotation of crews onto other vehicles. The narrow, official view saw the Duck as simply another truck, which any driver could handle. The result was that soldiers who'd never even rowed a boat, suddenly found themselves literally out of their depth, trying to beach a Duck in pounding surf, or manoeuvre alongside a ship in a heavy swell, while men carefully trained for such demanding work ended up wasting their time and their talents driving conventional trucks, far inland.

The clash of cultures between the Army and the Navy also continued to cause problems. As the fleet of landing craft of every shape and size grew steadily larger, so did the number of Soldiers-

THE 'A' FRAME

Typical of the spirit which first hatched the idea of the Duck, was the 'A' Frame crane. Ducks were designed to be loaded, whilst alongside a ship, by using its deck cranes. Unloading was not so easy. A conventional truck body has a drop-down tail-gate to simplify loading and unloading. But, since the Duck was effectively a boat, the load had to be lifted out of its hold: an impossible task with a heavy item, like a field gun – unless there was a crane. To speed up the process, small items were transported in cargo nets, which also needed unloading by crane. But in war, things have a habit of not going to plan and the Ducks often struggled ashore only to find there were no cranes to unload them.

In a moment of inspired improvisation, the spirit of the frontiersman rose to the challenge. A Duck crew rigged up their own crane, using two long timbers and the winch that every Duck carried on its rear deck. Lashed together at one end and mounted on the rear deck, splayed apart, the timbers formed a pair of sheer-legs. Braced by stays and cables, they stood on the deck like a giant letter 'A'. The winch cable was run through a pulley, mounted at the top of the frame, and could be used to lift surprisingly heavy items. The 'Crane Duck' could not unload itself, but could be positioned to unload others.

The Army quickly saw the value of this device and from September 1943, a factory-made version using metal tubes became a standard item of Duck equipment. Although the Duck was never intended to be a crane and its use for this task reduced the number in use for transport, it was a lot better than nothing. During landings in the south of France, a failure to provide enough cranes meant that about 25% of the Ducks were tied up unloading the rest. Even items as heavy as a 105mm howitzer, or a 4,000lb bomb could be handled by the 'A' frame.

turned-Sailors. Soon the Army owned more boats than the Navy, which became increasingly touchy about the erosion of its traditional role. At least the Duck was only half a boat, but the Navy still showed a reluctance to co-operate with the Army on its use, believing that it had to be a boat really. The debate rarely produced open hostility, but it was often counter-productive. Sailors looking down on army Duck crews, struggling with ropes and fenders to hold position alongside their ships, tended to have little sympathy for their lack of seamanship. Who did these landlubbers think they were kidding?

But the Duck crews could give as good as they got. The following exchange is said to have taken place during the landing at Anzio in Italy:

Duck Driver: *'I'm not taking that load, its too big!'*
Ship's officer: *'I order you to take this load!'*
Duck Driver: *'Yeah? And who are you?'*
Ship's officer: *'I'm the First Mate of this ship damn it, now get back alongside!'*
Duck Driver: *'In your eye! I'm the Captain of this here Duck, and you can keep a civil tongue in your head when talking to your superiors.'*

Another divergence of opinion existed between the Army and the Marines. While the Army readily adopted the Duck as a clever modification of its GMC truck, some Marines were less enthusiastic

The DUKW first went into action in the Pacific, its unmistakable outline can be seen in this action picture of marines taking cover just above the waterline on a Japanese-held island in the Marianas.

and preferred their own purpose-built landing vehicle, the Landing Vehicle Tracked, or LVT. It resembled a large tank hull and could actually be fitted with a gun turret and armour plate, turning it into a tank in all but name. Like the Duck, it could swim ashore and drive up the beach: unlike the Duck, it soon acquired a suitably robust name – the 'Buffalo'. Comparisons with the Duck were inevitable and, since both had their strengths and weaknesses, neither of the rivals emerged as the clear winner.

The Buffalo could carry three tons of supplies and one version had a ramp, to assist the process of unloading. Being a tracked vehicle, it was better able to cope with sharp rocks and soft sand, but the tracks limited its road speed to 25 mph, half that of the Duck. The Buffalo represented another approach to the amphibian, taking the landing craft rather than the truck as its starting point. It played an important role during the Pacific island landings and more than 18,000 were built. But it was less seaworthy than the Duck and of very limited use on land.

Rod Stephens was concerned to ensure that the crews used the Ducks efficiently and spent most of his time touring round the training camps. He stressed the importance of keeping the Ducks properly maintained and protecting them from the ravages of salt water and sand. He was also keen to impress on the crews that the versatility of the Duck should not be abused by driving for long distances inland.

The British public gets its very first look at the Buffalo ('rival' to the DUKW) in this press photograph dated Oct 30th, 1944.

Sitting in traffic jams, miles from the ships it was meant to be unloading, would not be an efficient use of the amphibian. As the battlefront moved further inland, it would increasingly limit the Duck's usefulness if most of its time was spent away from its intended sphere of operation, the beach. It would then become essential to trans-ship the load into normal trucks.

As the Allied production of war material got into top gear, the sheer scale of the operation became awe inspiring. As the convoys of mass-produced 'Liberty Ships' ploughed to and fro across the Atlantic, vast stockpiles of supplies were assembled in Britain in preparation for an invasion of Europe. It became a standard joke among the armed forces that the only thing which stopped the island sinking under the weight, was the forest of barrage balloons, protecting vulnerable targets from low level air attacks. One sailor described the country as being buried under war material and took the time to list what he'd seen.

> *'Everywhere were lined up jeeps, tanks, trucks, half-tracks, and ambulances. Rations, canned goods, cannons, machine guns, rifles, pistols, ammunition, bombs, hand grenades, mines, mortars, uniforms, clothing, medicine, bandages, ointment, plasma, drugs, gasoline, kerosene, diesel fuel and hundreds of other necessary items were stacked in cans, boxes, barrels, drums, kegs and cartons.'*

There were many others he didn't mention, like the tools and the mountains of spare parts needed to keep the machines running. These

General Montgomery acknowledges a salute from British soldiers in Sicily, July 1943. He is riding in a Duck belonging to the 51st (Highland) Division.

many thousands of items would form the cargo that any invading army would have to take to France and land on its beaches, if the war was to be won. The same process would have to be performed on the other invasion fronts, from North Africa to Okinawa.

The first large-scale use of the Duck was during operation 'Husky', the Invasion of Sicily, launched on 10 July 1943. The British, under General Montgomery, landed on the east coast with 300 Ducks. The Americans, under General Patton, landed with 700 in the south. Other new landing craft, designed for bringing tanks ashore, were also seen in action for the first time and the initial operation was regarded as highly successful. There was little opposition from the Italians and the Germans were not able to mount a major counter-attack quickly enough. But the weather then began to deteriorate and it was the Ducks that really saved the day. Many of the larger landing craft beached on sandbars well away from the shore and were unable to unload until causeways had been constructed to reach them. Although unable to unload the tanks, the Ducks were able to run a constant shuttle operation, acting as ferries for men and equipment. One was recorded as having carried ashore a load of 7 tons – almost three times its design weight.

By the third day of the invasion, 90% of all cargoes were coming ashore by Duck. Wounded men were ferried out on the return trips, along with prisoners. Despite all the training, many of the Ducks were driven far inland as the invading troops advanced and twenty of them were actually captured by the Germans during a counter-attack!

DUCK CREWS

Both the Americans and the British formed special Duck Companies: a British Company consisted of 132 Ducks and 470 men. The Americans used a smaller unit of fifty Ducks, operated by 173 enlisted men, under seven officers. The British units were mostly trained to a much higher standard, particularly on the mechanical side, and they proved to be far better at keeping their vehicles running under combat conditions. Four days after the start of the landings at Anzio in Italy, 14% of British Ducks were listed as unserviceable, the American figure was 55%.

Part of the problem was an ingrained attitude within the American High Command to Negro soldiers. Segregation of U.S. forces was surprisingly rigid in World War Two, even among units formed in the northern states. In the Deep South, anti Negro feeling ran very deep and segregation was firmly enforced in civilian life and in the military. The Civil War was still a bitter memory for a lot of Americans and many in the south chose to see the Negro as its cause. The soldier of 1943, could have listened as a child, to his grandparent's vivid stories of the slaughter at Gettysburg or Sherman's infamous looting spree through Georgia in the 1860s.

The most common way to segregate black G.I.s was to place them in non-combatant units, like catering, supply and transport. Many ended up in Duck operating companies, but their training was often minimal, thanks to a commonly held view that they simply wouldn't be able to grasp the technicalities of the machine. This attitude, which today would be firmly outlawed as blatant racism, was rarely challenged despite the fact that, when given proper training, black Duck drivers performed just as well as their white counterparts.

When the landings were completed, the Ducks were driven across the island, ready for the next assault, across the Straits of Messina. They soon became the most popular form of troop transport as their hulls provided much better protection against exploding landmines than the floor of a conventional truck. General Eisenhower was profoundly impressed by the performance of these new amphibians, which he later described as 'one of the most valuable pieces of equipment produced by the United States during the war'. His glowing report to Washington stated: 'Amphibious truck, two and one-half ton, commonly called DUKW, has been invaluable. Suggest commendation for officer responsible for its development.' He was not aware at the time that the Army's only part in the project had been to oppose it. His wholehearted support for the amphibian meant that its future was assured in any further landings. Some senior officers even expressed the opinion that Operation 'Husky' could well have failed without the Ducks.

Having crossed Sicily by road, the hundreds of Ducks were able to easily swim the two miles across the Straits of Messina and drive on up the Italian mainland to rendezvous with the next seaborne landing on 9th September at Salerno, twenty miles south of Naples. The Italian people were by now heartily sick of the war – and of the Germans, who were behaving more like an occupying power than an ally. The Fascist Dictator, Benito Mussolini, would soon be overthrown and

DUKWs leaving an LST in Salerno harbour.

later executed by Partisans. Italy withdrew from the war the day before the Salerno landings, leaving the battle-hardened German troops to face the Allied invasion alone.

The Salerno landings were far less straightforward than Sicily. German heavy armour was soon on the scene and resistance was determined. Many of the initial landings were beaten back, while the Ducks ended up circling off-shore, unable to deliver their loads. When they did eventually get ashore, there were not enough trucks available to trans-ship their cargoes into and the Ducks again saved the day by driving direct from the ships to the battlefield. It demonstrated their versatility, but slowed down the rate of unloading.

After three weeks, the port of Naples was captured, but the retreating Germans made sure that none of the quays or other port installations survived for the Allies to make use of. Once more the Duck provided the answer. A fleet of 600 was assembled to unload the supply ships, which could at least shelter in the harbour. Endlessly shuttling between the ships and the shore, the Ducks managed to unload some 3,500 tons per day, almost half the total handled by the fully operational port before the war.

The next major assault, in January 1944, captured the Italian port of Anzio intact and the Duck's talents were less crucial to the operation's success, since many ships were able to discharge in the normal way directly onto the quays. But five months later the crucial invasion of France would see the Ducks back in the thick of the action. 'Operation Overlord' was the greatest amphibious operation in history and the

INSTRUCTION PLATES

One positive step towards making the Duck less daunting, was the generous provision of instruction plates for the drivers. Signs gave helpful information on almost every aspect of Duck operation: how to enter the water, deal with waves, avoid getting stuck, prevent fires, set tyre pressures, operate the winch and keep the engine from overheating. There were plates giving detailed information on cold weather precautions, the correct use of gears and their optimum speeds, even the care of brake linings. When the surf deflector plate was raised, a sign was revealed reminding the driver to check his tyre pressures before landing. Nothing was left to chance.

BEFORE WATER ENTRY CLOSE 4 HULL DRAIN VALVES, CHECK 3 BOTTOM & 3 SHAFT TUBE DRAIN PLUGS

FOR SAND – SET TIRES AT 10#, ENGAGE FRONT WHEELS, USE LOW RANGE 2ND GEAR, FULL THROTTLE. STEER COURSE AT RIGHT ANGLE TO WAVES. MAINTAIN FULL THROTTLE CLEAR ACROSS BEACH. IF PROGRESS STOPS, CUT POWER IMMEDIATELY. NEVER ALLOW WHEELS TO DIG IN. IF STOPPED MOSTLY IN WATER, BACK FULL THROTTLE UNTIL WELL CLEAR AND TRY BETTER SPOT. IF STOPPED MOSTLY CLEAR OF WATER, WINCH SELF FORWARD. WHEN STUCK IN SURF, RIG TARPAULIN IMMEDIATELY AND KEEP PUMPS GOING.

FOR CORAL OR SHARP ROCK – SET TIRES AT 30#, ENGAGE FRONT WHEELS, USE LOW RANGE 2ND GEAR, AVOID LARGE BOULDERS AND NIGGER HEADS. OPERATE AT PART THROTTLE, 3 TO 4 MILES PER HOUR.

ALWAYS AVOID MUD, SWAMPS, WEED PATCHES, JAGGED ROCKS, LARGE BOULDERS AND STUMPS.

statistics still seem almost unbelievable: 5,000 ships, 175,000 troops, 1,500 tanks, 11,000 aircraft and of course 2,000 Ducks. At dawn, on 6 June 1944, the first waves began landing on the beaches of Normandy. Despite heavy losses among some of the Allied forces, particularly the Americans at Omaha beach, the operation was a triumphant success.

But there were plenty of problems along the way. The weather was not good and there was a heavy swell running as the landing craft hit the beaches, many of the assault troops were violently seasick and even the regular sailors found it tough going. For the Duck crews it was a very risky business: trying to hold position while loading men and equipment alongside the big ships, they were battered against their hulls or crashed into other landing craft – or each other, as the heaving waters of the English Channel flung them up and down.

Once ashore, the firm sand of the Normandy beaches provided ideal operating conditions for the Ducks, which once more set about doing the job that Rod Stephens and his team had designed them for. In a never-ending circuit, they would load, swim to shore, unload and swim back to the supply ship. When it was empty they would move on to the next one. Soon it became a two-way traffic, as the Ducks brought in supplies and evacuated the wounded. Until the gigantic, prefabricated 'Mulberry' harbours could be established, the Ducks worked without stopping and carried roughly 40% of the daily

Ferrying supplies from the transports to the beach. It required a degree of skill to operate alongside the big ships in a heavy swell.

average of 14,500 tons of supplies brought ashore. When a violent storm destroyed the American harbour on 18th June, the Ducks again worked round the clock to save the situation.

On 27th June, the port of Cherbourg was captured. But, as at Naples, the Germans first destroyed all the port's cranes and other facilities, to ensure that it could not be used by the Allies. And, as at Naples, the Ducks had the answer. Rounded up from the beach-heads they were driven to Cherbourg and set to work unloading the fleets of Liberty ships that now poured men and equipment into the battle. In the month following D-Day, a million men, half a million tons of supplies and more than 171,000 vehicles were landed in France.

At the end of July, Operation Cobra was launched. General Patton's Third Army broke out to the south west of the invasion beaches and began a rapid outflanking of the German forces. Soon his supply lines were becoming dangerously overstretched and shortage of fuel supplies became a growing problem. Nobody had predicted such a rapid advance. C-47 transport aircraft managed to deliver large quantities of fuel, but at a high cost in men and machines shot down. The railway system lay in ruins as the result of Allied bombing, so road haulage was the only option.

The Transportation Corps quickly organised a system of non-stop road convoys. It was christened the 'Red Ball Express' and followed

The DUKW was used in large numbers to ferry men and equipment to and from the D-Day landing beaches on the Normandy coast. The tarpaulin covers are rigged, usually a sign that casualties are being evacuated.

specially reserved routes through the French countryside. The narrow lanes of Normandy were not considered suitable for two-way traffic, so the 'Express' operated as a gigantic one-way circuit. It was worked by a huge fleet of trucks including almost 6,000 GMCs. At Cherbourg, the floating version of the truck would swim out to a Liberty ship, moored in the harbour. Waddling out of the water, via specially built ramps, the Duck would stop under a crane and transfer its load to a 'Red Ball' truck. As the empty Duck returned to the ship, a full one took its place under the crane and the next empty truck pulled up for its load.

The entire operation was living proof of the triumph of American mass-production over impossible odds. The first link in the chain was the pre-fabricated Liberty ship. Each one weighed over 10,000 tons and 2,700 of them were built. Each could carry about 9,000 tons of fuel and cargo and surviving even one Atlantic crossing was regarded as sufficient to justify the cost of its construction. Then came the Duck, one of over 20,000 built. It took about 4,500 round trips to empty one Liberty ship. Finally came the Duck's half-brother, the GMC truck. The 'Red Ball' fleet of trucks in action was an awe-inspiring sight, strung out along the French roads in an unbroken line of supply, stretching as far as the eye could see. Yet it represented less than one percent of the total production run of almost 600,000.

Two-way traffic. Loaded DUKWs on the right head inland, while the empties on the left return to the water. Note the partly torn-off fenders and dented hull on the nearest vehicle.

Running the 'Red Ball Express' was an exhausting job for the drivers and the vehicles. The trucks were battering the overloaded road system into a mass of ruts and potholes, wearing out hundreds of tyres in the process every day, as well as gulping some 200,000 gallons of fuel. By the middle of November, when the operation ended, most of the trucks and Ducks were simply worn out by non-stop work. But their mission had been achieved. As the rail links were restored, the 'G.I.' steam engines of the Transportation Corps – also mass-produced in America – were able to deliver ten times the 'Red Ball' tonnage as the Allied advance continued.

Half a world away from the bitter fighting in France, the American

Keeping up the pressure. The Red Ball drivers were urged on by signs and slogans – and by the ever-present military police.

forces were engaged in a series of successful amphibious landings as they 'island hopped' their way across the Pacific. As they neared Japan, resistance became more determined and the battles became more bloody. Ducks were used in most of the operations with varying degrees of success, mostly depending on how well they were handled. One of the many instruction plates in the cab advised the driver on what tyre pressure to use in a range of conditions. 30lb was the recommended pressure for operating on the sharp coral spikes of the Pacific island reefs. The sign included the stern warning to *'always avoid mud, swamps, weed patches, jagged rocks, large boulders and stumps.'* Even the Duck apparently had its limitations, as the Americans would find to their cost on a tiny volcanic island called Iwo Jima.

Situated just 660 miles from Tokyo, Iwo Jima was seen as a possible base for airborne operations against the mainland of Japan. But the Japanese defenders were well dug into their defensive positions and determined to defend the island to the last man, which is almost exactly what they did. The fanaticism that drove more than 20,000 soldiers to die for their Emperor rather than surrender, was an alien and disturbing phenomenon to the easy-going G.I. But the cost in American lives was also high, 6,821 men were killed, almost all of them Marines.

Iwo Jima has become part of American folklore, it produced perhaps the best known image of the war in the Pacific – the famous

Under the eyes of the Japanese defenders on Mount Suribachi, amphibious craft circle a US battleship prior to lining up for their run in to the beaches.

photograph of the victorious Marines raising the Stars and Stripes on Mount Suribachi (see p216). It caught the spirit of the moment and helped to confirm America's belief in its cause. The conviction that the 'American way' is the right way was also embodied in another icon, the actor John Wayne. His laconic style seemed to express the things which Americans wanted to believe about themselves. He projected the image of a nation of un-complicated idealists: men of few words, slow to anger but tough and determined fighters when roused. Typical of the breed is his character in the film 'Sands of Iwo Jima', which helped the American people to come to terms with one of the most traumatic battles of World War Two.

The film takes its title from the black volcanic ash, which forms the Iwo Jima beaches. Its very blackness seemed to re-enforce for the American troops the feeling of entering an alien and hostile world as they lay, pinned down by a hail of crossfire. But it would be its texture that remained most clearly in the memory. It was quite unlike the firm sand of the Normandy beaches, being deep and soft, piled high on beaches which sloped steeply up from the water's edge. It was hard to walk on and almost impossible to drive on. Inaccurate intelligence reports had indicated that the landing conditions would be good, with firm sand suitable for amphibians. But what the Marines actually encountered could hardly have been worse.

Iwo Jima is dominated by the dormant volcano Mount Suribachi,

In a sea of black sand, below Mount Suribachi, a DUKW unloads supplies. The Marines had great difficulty in moving stores inland from the steeply shelved and unstable dunes of volcanic ash.

which once spewed out the black ash that forms its beaches. From this vantage point, the Japanese defenders had a commanding field of fire. After an initial naval bombardment, the Marines moved in and just after 9am on 19 February 1945, the first wave of landing craft hit the beaches. They were accompanied by 'Buffalo' tracked amphibians, which attempted to claw their way onto the fine ash. Many failed and became marooned at the water's edge, where they were rapidly swamped by the surf. The Japanese had constructed an elaborate system of underground tunnels and bunkers, which resisted most of the effects of the bombardment. Now they emerged to saturate the landing beaches with lethal crossfire. As the American troops struggled ashore, they suffered heavy losses.

At Iwo Jima, Duck crews faced some of the toughest conditions ever encountered during amphibious operations. Three companies were composed of Negro soldiers who had been properly trained by O.S.R.D. instructors. Many of the drivers were praised later for their skill and courage under fire. One ran out of fuel and drifted for thirteen hours, but refused to abandon his machine when passing landing craft offered to take him ashore. He was eventually towed in, with his Duck and its cargo intact. By contrast, the two (all-white) Marine units, which had not been given special training in handling the Duck, suffered very heavy losses.

The prize. American troops survey the churned-up wasteland of volcanic ash that cost so many lives to win.

The Marines planned to bring artillery ashore by Duck. Twelve heavy 105mm howitzers were craned into twelve Ducks, lined up inside one of the large landing ships. But they were dangerously overloaded for the rough sea conditions and as each Duck was driven down the bow ramp of the landing ship and into the sea, it quickly filled with water and sank. Only four of the twelve managed to reach the shore, where two more were swamped by the breakers. Only two guns were left to use against the defenders. More Ducks began coming ashore with ammunition, but because the beach sloped so steeply they could only get their front wheels ashore, which spun helplessly and quickly buried themselves in the ash. Unable to move up the beach, the Ducks would soon swing broadside to the waves and be swamped. The beach quickly became a jumble of stranded landing craft and amphibians, wallowing in the breakers and hampering further landings.

At a few points, the beach was less steeply sloped and by lowering their tyre pressures to a mere 5 pounds per square inch, the Ducks managed to clamber ashore. By nightfall on the first day, 30,000 troops had been landed and were holding a beachhead 3,000 yards long. For three days, the Marines clawed their way up Mount Suribachi. The Japanese fought to the death for every yard of ground and showed no willingness to surrender. Only by wiping out the defenders in their foxholes and tunnels, were the Marines able to advance. On the

TYRES

One problem with beach operations is traction. Sand can be a very variable medium. When wet, it can be almost as firm as a concrete slab. But, under certain conditions, it can lose its solidity and become treacherous quick sand. When dry, it is blown by the wind into dunes, which can be difficult enough to climb on foot, let alone to drive up. The grip exerted by a pneumatic tyre can be improved by lowering the air pressure. Tests established that the Duck performed best on soft sand or mud with a pressure of 10lb per square inch. For severe conditions, 5lb was recommended. One of the great advantages of the Duck was its ability to instantly become a 50mph road vehicle, on clearing the beach. But running at speed on a paved road with flat tyres would soon wreck them. The best pressure for road use was 40lb, but stopping to re-inflate the tyres when leaving the beach would be a waste of precious time and really could turn the stranded amphibian into a 'sitting duck' for the enemy to shoot at.

Undaunted, the design team invented a solution to the problem. From December 1943 onwards, Ducks were fitted with a central tyre inflation system. A compressor, driven from the engine, fed air to all six tyres via the wheel hubs. On each wheel, the tyre valve was linked by a short tube to a round chamber mounted on the hub. The chamber was in two halves, able to rotate independently while maintaining an air-tight seal. So, while one half rotated with the wheel, the other half remained static and was fixed to an air pipe, mounted on the hull and fed by the compressor.

Using this system, a Duck could swim ashore and clamber up a soft sandy beach using low tyre pressures. Then, as it reached a paved road, pressure could be increased without stopping. When it went off-road, or returned to the beach, the tyre pressure could be reduced once more. The system was not ideal: the air pipes were exposed and easily damaged by rough handling, but it did work and had the unexpected advantage of making the tyres virtually bullet-proof. Tests revealed that tyres which had several shots fired into them could still be kept inflated by running the compressor continuously.

morning of the fifth day of the invasion, they reached the top and raised the Stars and Stripes.

Meanwhile, the surviving Ducks were playing a key role in the transport of vital supplies like ammunition, but the sands of Iwo Jima had tested them to the very limit: more than 50% of the Ducks were lost in the first five days. The whole island was eventually captured after almost a month of bitter fighting. It was one of the toughest battles ever fought by American troops and the losses in men and equipment were devastating. Twenty seven Medals of Honour were awarded, the highest number for any single operation in World War

The Stars and Stripes fly over Iwo Jima. A potent image of team work and patriotism that has become a part of American folklore.

Two. The exact number of Japanese defenders was never established, some estimates put it as high as 23,000, but barely 200 survived to be taken prisoner.

When the war finally ended, the Duck and the GMC truck both continued to serve in the military. In the Korean War, they still played their part. They never achieved the status of superstars – the fighters and the bombers, the tanks and the big guns would always grab the headlines – but time after time, it was the humble transports which helped to tip the balance in the Allies' favour during amphibious operations in World War Two. Study a picture of the D-Day landings that shows troops pouring ashore, or tanks rolling to victory, and there is a good chance that a 'Duck' or a 'Jimmy' will be in the background, usually ignored in the caption. General Eisenhower, the Supreme Allied Commander, was one who fully understood their value. After the final victory, he identified five items of unarmed equipment that were among the most vital contributors to Allied success. They were the bulldozer, the Jeep, the two and a half ton truck, the C47 aircraft and the Duck.

Every war needs its heroes, symbolic figures who are willing to fight and die for the cause. When it's all over, they are immortalised in stone and bronze – and on celluloid. Standing proudly above memorials to their fallen comrades, gallant soldiers thrust their bayonets at the sky, heroic Generals on horseback brandish swords, the victorious G.I.s march on as the music swells and the credits roll. But where are the movies and the monuments to honour the crane operator, or the Duck driver? Since they go to war without weapons, they are classed as 'non combatants' and are usually denied their fair share of the glory. They may take extraordinary risks to deliver their precious cargo under fire, but their image is just not 'heroic' enough to capture the public imagination. Like the water supply or the telephone, transport is taken for granted, until it stops. When the tap runs dry, or the phone goes dead – or the tank advance is halted for lack of fuel – there is an outcry.

Many involved in keeping the military on the move, felt their contribution was only noticed when they failed to deliver and morale suffered accordingly. If the operation went smoothly and the victory was won, largely thanks to their efforts, they were usually overlooked when the citations were being handed out. The supply chain always seems to be part of 'The Forgotten Army', however vital its part in the action and however much the Generals may acknowledge its importance. And yet it often held the key to victory. The old proverb still applied, even when tyres and trucks had replaced shoes and horses.

> *For the want of a nail, the shoe was lost.*
> *For the want of a shoe, the horse was lost.*
> *For the want of a horse, the rider was lost.*
> *For the want of a rider, the battle was lost.*
> *For the want of a battle, the Kingdom was lost.*
> *And all for the want of a horse-shoe nail.*

On the Bosworth battlefield, Shakespeare's Richard III offers his Kingdom for a horse, so transport clearly meant a lot to him. There were times when a single Duck would have been worth a whole troupe of horses, but no general is on record as having offered to trade his stars for one.

There were brief moments of glory however. When the Allies were firmly ashore in Normandy, British Prime Minister Winston Churchill was given a guided tour of the D-Day beaches in a Duck. After four years in exile, the leader of the Free French Army, General De Gaulle, returned in triumph. His historic first step onto the newly-liberated soil of his native land was a deeply significant moment for the people of France. That step was made from a Duck – not very dignified perhaps, but very practical. Later it was agreed that King George VI should cross the Channel, to set the seal on the victory. The problem of getting him from the ship to the shore, while still keeping the Royal feet dry, was solved in the obvious way. Flanked by Admirals of the Fleet, he rode ashore in state – in a Duck.

POSTSCRIPT

With the Atomic Bomb, the nature of warfare changed for ever. When one aircraft can deliver a single bomb that wipes out an entire city, mass-production on the scale seen in World War Two becomes unnecessary. The emphasis now is on fewer, far more sophisticated and vastly more expensive, conventional weapons. The days of building fighter planes by the thousand, or trucks by the hundred thousand are probably consigned to the scrapyard of history, along with the broadsword and the cavalry charge.

But there still remains a vast storehouse of these machines, which survive exactly as they left the factory in the 1940s. Engines that have never been started, guns that have never fired a shot, aircraft that have never flown, are still coated with grease and packed in their crates, along with their despatch notes and instruction manuals. They lie at the bottom of the ocean, crowded into the holds of the great armada of cargo ships lost in action. Deep down in the Atlantic, far from the light of day and the corrosive effects of oxygen, they share the sea bed with the wrecks of the German U-Boats that sank them and the bones of the thousands who lost their lives. Across the world, the ocean floor is littered with the wreckage of war: gigantic battleships and small coasters, destroyers and troopships, freighters and landing craft, submarines and aircraft carriers. They rest with the countless other wrecks of ships lost since man first went to sea. Most of them are uncharted but they are still there waiting to be found.

They represent a gigantic stockpile of raw materials: hundreds of millions of tons of precious bronze, copper, nickel and brass; of steel, aluminium, coal, oil, rubber and all the other ingredients of mechanised warfare. Many of these resources are finite and one day man may have to reap this harvest. As the technology of marine salvage advances, who knows how many Spitfires, Sherman Tanks, C47s, GMC trucks and Ducks may rise from the deep? And what will future generations make of them? Raising the wreck of Henry VIII's ship the Mary Rose has given a new insight into Tudor England. In the distant future, a fully loaded Liberty Ship could be an equally valuable treasure-house of information: mute evidence of global conflict on an epic scale.

The durability of many of the wartime designs means that even the ones which went into service and saw action, still survive in surprisingly large numbers. Some are in museums, others are lovingly restored to their original condition by enthusiasts. But the ones with peacetime uses, notably the C-47 aircraft and the GMC truck, are still earning their living, mostly in the Third World. Produced under wartime conditions and expected to last a matter of months, they have now outlived many of the men and women who built them. Patched and modified, abused and neglected, they soldier on. Some are barely recognisable as military equipment, but scrape beneath the surface and you'll find the same Government Issue olive drab. They are working reminders of an extraordinary moment in history, when mass-produced machines decided the future of the world.

INDEX

Spitfire fighter
pages 10 - 80